Bible 101

A Do-It-Yourself User's Guide

by Wes Haystead

STANDARD
PUBLISHING
Cincinnati, Ohio

The Standard Publishing Company, Cincinnati, Ohio
A division of Standex International Corporation
© 1996 by Wesley Haystead
All rights reserved
Printed in the United States of America

03   02   01   00   99   98   97   96   5   4   3   2   1

Editing, design, and cover by settingPace, LLC.

Library of Congress Cataloging-in-Publication Data

Haystead. Wesley.
   Bible 101 : a do-it-yourself user's guide / by Wes Haystead.
     p.   cm.
  ISBN 0-7847-0454-6
  1. Bible--Study and teaching.   2. Bible--Introductions.
 I. Title.
 BS600.2.H37   1996   96-7302
 220'.07--dc20   CIP

CONTENTS

LESSON 1   **1**
A Look at the Book

LESSON 2   **23**
The Books of History

LESSON 3   **41**
The Poets and Prophets

LESSON 4   **57**
The Life of Jesus

LESSON 5   **71**
The Growth of the Church

LESSON 6   **93**
Letters to Churches

FOR REFERENCE
How Did We Get the Bible?   *105*
Glossary   *111*

THE BIBLE: EASY ACCESS GUIDE
Pull-out Booklet

INTRODUCTION

BUILDING BIBLE STUDY SKILLS
by Wes Haystead

This six-session study introduces adults to the structure, content, and message of the Bible. The reader is introduced to each of the main sections of the Bible as well as carefully selected events, characters, themes, and passages from Scripture.

This study provides simple, practical guidance. It will help readers locate references, find information on topics of interest, and begin a productive, personal Bible reading plan. Balancing the presentation of mechanics for finding one's way within the Bible are a variety of useful approaches to gaining personal spiritual benefit from Bible reading.

At the end of the manual is a handy pull-out booklet, *The Bible: Easy Access Guide.* This concise guide can be kept inside the reader's Bible for quick reference.

This manual is more than just a book about studying the Bible. It guides the student in actual Bible study experiences. Each lesson takes about 60–75 minutes to complete. The manual is designed for both the individual studying alone and for participants in a study group (Sunday morning, electives, home Bible group, etc.). Each lesson contains guidance suggestions for a group leader.

LESSON 1

A Look at the Book

A group of children was asked, "Why is the Bible special?" Hands shot up, and a diverse stream of "becauses" was blurted out:

"Because it's big."

"Because it's got a black cover."

"Mine has a white cover. It's because there's gold lettering on it."

"Mine has silver lettering. It's because it says 'Holy Bible.'"

"Mine says 'Children's Bible.' It's because the pages have gold edges."

The children had focused on the physical appearance of the Bibles they had seen. This lesson takes you beyond the surface to explore the essential features that make the Bible a unique and treasured book.

LESSON 1—A LOOK AT THE BOOK

OUTLINE

- Why Study Such an Old Book Today?
- Finding Your Way Around
- What Kind of Book Is This?
- Where Do I Start?—Choosing What to Study First

LEARNING ACTIVITIES

❏ Throughout this lesson you will find a variety of helpful learning activities indicated by a check box ❏. Mark the check box when you complete each activity.

LESSON TIME: 60–75 minutes

Leader Notes

> If guiding a group in studying this course together, see the instructions and tips for guiding the group sessions that appear in boxes such as this one.

10–15 MINUTES **INTO THE LESSON**

Some Things I'd Like to Know

> "I shot an arrow into the air; it fell to earth, I knew not where."—*Henry Wadsworth Longfellow*

This familiar bit of poetry describes how many of us tend to approach learning situations. We attend the class sessions, or we read the book, but often we have little or no idea in mind of what we expect to learn through the process. As a result, most of us can look back on courses we've taken and books we've read with only a vague or limited sense of what we really learned from the effort expended.

❑ To avoid repeating that pattern with this course, pause for a few minutes before you start exploring the content of this lesson. Make a thoughtful list of what you hope to gain from this study. What are some things about the Bible that you want to know? List them on the blank lines shown below.

Leader Notes

Before the session, mount a large sheet of newsprint or butcher paper on a wall near the front of the room. Have ready some marking pens. As participants arrive, welcome them and invite them to list on the paper some things they hope to learn about the Bible as a result of participating in this course. Instruct them to read what the others have written, and add their initials to any statements already written that describe something they also want to learn. Encourage people to introduce themselves to others in the group whom they do not already know.

_____

_____

_____

_____

_____

Leader Notes

As people complete writing statements, read aloud what participants have written that they want to learn about the Bible. Invite volunteers to share reasons why people want to know these things. Add these reasons to the paper. Write in large letters and use a distinctive marker color, or draw a bold circle around each reason.

Why I Want to Know These Things About the Bible

❑ List reasons why you want to know more about the Bible. What benefits do you hope to gain from the things you will learn?

_____

_____

_____

_____

> **Leader Notes**
>
> Lead the group in prayer, asking God to help each participant learn what God wants each person to know about his Word.

40–45 MINUTES INTO THE WORD

The Bible has long been the most widely distributed book in the world, and has been translated into more languages than any other. But it has also been called "the world's least-read best-seller." Your interest in learning how to study the Bible will keep that description from being true in your own life.

10 MINUTES **Step 1:   Why Study Such an Old Book Today?**

Its Remarkable Claims.   The Bible is not shy about making startling claims for itself. It repeatedly asserts that it is unique, both in the kind of book it is, and in the impact reading it will have in people's lives.

❑ Read the declarations on **Worksheet 1.1 (p. 17)**, then write a reason why each one is a significant reason to study the Bible.

> **Leader Notes**
>
> Divide participants into pairs or trios. Assign each small group one or two of the Scriptures to read, and then discuss together why that statement is a valid reason to study the Bible. After several minutes, invite volunteers to share their verses and reasons.

The Testimonials of Others.   There are many reasons to accept the claims Scripture makes for itself. One of the most persuasive is that an amazingly large and diverse crowd of people over the centuries has told of the powerful ways the Bible has impacted their lives. Such an army of "satisfied customers" is not to be taken lightly.

❑ Select two quotations from the list on **Worksheet 1.2 (p. 18)** that you find most persuasive in encouraging you to study the Bible. Write a statement telling why these quotations appeal to you.

Share with the group one positive benefit you have gained from your own study of Scripture. Then invite volunteers to read aloud the quotations on Worksheet 1.2. After participants mark the two quotations they find most persuasive and write a sentence telling what they like about those quotations, ask volunteers to read aloud the sentences they wrote.

The Timelessness of Its Message. Might it be that a book written in the ancient world, before the age of space exploration, instant worldwide communication, personal computers, laser surgery, and beach volleyball, might not have much to say to people in today's culture? May it be that the Bible is no longer worth the time and energy its study requires?

If the Bible were merely the product of its human authors, the product of devout—even brilliant—authors who lived in ancient Palestine during momentous historical events, the answer would be "yes." The Bible would be relegated to study by a few scholars drawn to arcane topics.

Instead, the Bible speaks as forcefully to people today as in any age, dealing with the unchanging issues of human nature and God's objectives for his creation. We are often taken up with the surface changes in human life, yet God's Word continues to reveal insights about our deepest needs and desires in light of his plans for us.

With people in the same small groups as earlier, assign each group one or two of the Scriptures on Worksheet 1.3. Instruct them to work together. After several minutes of interaction, invite volunteers to share insights gained about the value of the Bible in today's world.

❑ Consider each of the affirmations listed on **Worksheet 1.3 (p. 19)** about the continuing value of God's Word. Then, alongside each verse, write one or more current issues that that verse calls to your mind as something Scripture effectively addresses.

Leader Notes

Show two or three translations you have enjoyed using. Briefly describe to the group what you like best about each one. Suggest a translation for group members to use during this course and for their personal Bible study.

NOTE: The Scriptures printed in this manual are from *The Holy Bible— New International Version*, unless otherwise noted.

A Few Notes About Translations

The Bible was originally written in Hebrew (Old Testament) and Greek (New Testament). Obviously, English readers depend on translations to be able to read God's Word for themselves. A great many translations are available, giving the reader choices that are sometimes confusing. In choosing a translation, consider these factors:

1. **Translation or Paraphrase?** No two languages exactly match up alongside one another with identical grammatical structures and paralleling vocabularies. Thus, different Bible versions vary as to how the translators chose to render the message from one language to the next. In general, translations (e.g., *Authorized [King James] Version, New Revised Version, New American Standard Version, New International Version*) attempt to stay as close to the original structure and vocabulary as possible. Other versions, called paraphrases (e.g., *The Living Bible, The Message, Today's English Version, Phillips Modern Language Version*), try to recast the original ideas in whatever ways are seen as most natural and understandable in the new language. The former are generally considered to be more accurate, while the latter are often more readable. Many people rely on a translation for their study needs and a paraphrase for devotional reading.

2. **Understanding Level.** Some translations are easier to understand than others for some readers. For example, the *Authorized (King James) Version* was written in the seventeenth century, and thus poses difficulties for readers not familiar with many terms no longer in use. Some recent translations provide one or more rating scales that define their difficulty level (e.g., eighth grade reading level).

3. **Readability/Style.** A translation may be simple to understand but not easy to read. Keeping all the sentences short and vocabulary simple can aid in understanding, but may also result in a "choppy" writing style that does not "flow" easily. If you are trying to choose between versions, read several paragraphs from each version being considered.

4. **Use by Others.** There is benefit in using the same version that is used by others with whom you study. Find out which version your pastor reads from in the worship services you attend. Which version does the leader of your Bible study group use during the sessions? While there can be rich benefit in comparing the wording of different translations, you will usually find it easier to follow Scripture readings, sermons, and group discussions if you have the same translation being used by the leader and most other group members. (Unless, of course, the leader is working from the original Greek or Hebrew and is translating "on the fly.")

In summary, the abundance of different translations, while confusing at first, is a great benefit to Bible readers. Determining which one to read is really a "win/win" choice, one in which you need not worry about going wrong.

---

10 MINUTES

Step 2: Finding Your Way Around

Thumbing through a Bible's pages can be intimidating. The Bible is long, and many of the names of books are unfamiliar and hard to pronounce. Here are a few tips to easily locate a place in the Bible.

1. **Know the "Address"**
   The Bible has been meticulously subdivided so that almost every sentence has its own unique "address" or reference. Three pieces of information are consistently used in referring to any location in the Bible:

   Book Name—the name of one of the sixty-six Bible books (e.g., Genesis, Psalms, Mark).

Chapter—Most Bible books (except for several very short ones) are divided into chapters. Chapter numbers appear at the top of each page and in large type within the text.

Verse—All chapters are divided into verses. A verse can be a sentence or part of a sentence. Verse numbers appear in small type in the body of the text, except for the first verse of a chapter. Most Bibles print the chapter number or the first letter of the first word in large type and omit the numeral "1."

Bible references are written with the book name first, then the chapter and verse numbers separated by a colon (e.g., Genesis 1:1).

❏ Locate Genesis 1:1 in the front of your Bible and see how the chapter and verse numbers are printed. Your Bible may provide some introductory material before the text of Genesis begins.

NOTE: The chapter and verse divisions were added long after the books were written. For the most part they are very helpful. Occasionally they break up a passage that should be read as a unit.

Leader Notes

Have everyone locate Genesis 1:1. If group members have Bibles with different formats, invite volunteers to describe the appearance of the first page of Genesis and any introductory pages that precede the text. For example, "My Bible has several paragraphs of background information about Genesis. Then, in boldface, there's a title just above the text, with a big number 1 inset along the margin."

2. **Use the Contents Page(s)**

Every Bible has a contents page near the beginning of it. The standard format lists all the books of the Bible in the order the books appear, showing the thirty-nine Old Testament books first, then the twenty-seven New Testament books.

Some Bibles also have an alphabetical contents page, listing all the books in order by name. This makes it easy to quickly locate a book in the list if you are unfamiliar with its general position in the Bible.

Leader Notes

Guide the group in locating the references listed below. Once everyone has found a reference, invite a volunteer to read the verse(s) aloud.

❑ In your Bible, locate these familiar Bible references. Practice using the contents page to find the books.

Old Testament

❑ Deuteronomy 6:4-6 (the book of Deuteronomy, chapter 6, verses 4 through 6)

❑ Psalm 23:1 (the book of Psalms, chapter 23, verse 1)

❑ Proverbs 3:5, 6 (the book of Proverbs, chapter 3, verses 5 and 6)

New Testament

❑ John 3:16 (the book of John, chapter 3, verse 16)

❑ Romans 6:23 (the book of Romans, chapter 6, verse 23)

❑ 1 Corinthians 13:4-6 (the first book of Corinthians, chapter 13, verses 4 through 6)

10–15 MINUTES **Step 3: What Kind of a Book Is This?**

A Unique Library. The Bible is more than a book. It is a library of books. Sixty-six books to be exact. And, like any good library, there is remarkable diversity in the kinds of books included.

History

Twenty-two of the books (that's one-third of the entire Bible) tell the story—His Story! Starting with the creation, the first seventeen books of the Old Testament tell the dramatic and often tragic story of God's dealings with his people, the Jews. (The first five of these books—Genesis through Deuteronomy—are called the Law or the Books of Moses.) It's in these books of history that you find the classic Bible stories that have captivated children and challenged adults for thousands of years:

• Noah Builds the Ark
• The Faith of Abraham and Sarah
• Rebekah: A Bride for Isaac
• The Rivalry Between Jacob and Esau
• Joseph: From Prison to Palace

- Moses Leads Israel out of Egypt
- Joshua the Conqueror
- The Judges: Deborah, Gideon, Samson, Samuel
- Ruth and Naomi
- The Kings: Saul, David, Solomon, Hezekiah, Josiah
- The Prophets: Elijah, Elisha, Isaiah, Jeremiah
- The End of Captivity: Ezra, Nehemiah, Esther

More than 400 years separate the final events of the Old Testament from the beginning New Testament event, the birth of Jesus. The first five books of the New Testament tell the story of Jesus' life, death, and resurrection, and then the exciting adventure of the explosive spread of the Good News! The first four books—the Gospels—give us four different accounts of Jesus' life. The fifth book—Acts—carries the story on through the ministries of Peter, Philip, and Paul.

Poetry

Five Old Testament books provide a varied treasure trove of magnificent Hebrew poetry: the epic tale of Job's suffering, the prayers and hymns of the Psalms, the attention-grabbing wisdom of Proverbs and Ecclesiastes, and the beautiful romance of Solomon's Song of Songs. People of all generations have found solace, encouragement, motivation, instruction, and pleasure in the beauty and insight of these literary masterpieces.

Prophecy

The last seventeen books of the Old Testament and the final book of the New Testament are messages from prophets. The prophets were men and women who spoke and wrote God's messages, sometimes giving warnings or promises of things to come. All the Old Testament books of prophecy were written during the events described in the last five historical books (2 Kings, 2 Chronicles, Ezra, Nehemiah, Esther).

The first five books of prophecy in the Old Testament are called the Major Prophets, because of the length of the three longer books: Isaiah,

Jeremiah, and Ezekiel. Lamentations is a book of poetry that is linked by theme, history, and tradition with the prophet Jeremiah. Daniel is half history and half prophecy and fits chronologically with Ezekiel.

The last twelve books of prophecy in the Old Testament are called the Minor Prophets because they are all short books. In ancient times, all twelve were commonly written on the same scroll and came to be thought of as a unit, although they were completely separate messages written under distinctly different circumstances.

The only book of prophecy in the New Testament (Revelation) records the dramatic visions of the apostle John, foreseeing the ultimate triumph of Christ over the current world order.

Correspondence

Twenty-one of the New Testament books are letters (epistles) that are filled with instructions and insights about the beliefs and practices of the earliest Christians.

The first nine letters (Romans through Thessalonians) were sent by the apostle Paul to churches in key cities in the eastern Mediterranean.

The next four letters (Timothy through Philemon) were written by Paul to individual leaders. The two letters to Timothy and the one to Titus are called Pastoral Letters because they deal with the oversight of congregations.

The last eight letters (Hebrews through Jude) are often called the General Letters because they were written to a wider audience rather than to specific churches or individuals. Also, they were written by various writers (e.g., James, Peter, John, Jude).

❏ On the charts on **Worksheet 1.4 (p. 20)**, match the names of at least five of the characters to the books in which their stories are found. The references listed alongside some of the books are clues that mention the characters in the list.

A Cohesive Story. In spite of being sixty-six separate books written by more than forty authors over a period of 1,500 years, the Bible tells one cohesive story: God's redemptive dealings with people. This great story has many subplots, but the focus consistently remains on God's master plan for his creation. Throughout both the Old and New Testaments, we see God's purpose clearly stated.

❑ Read the verses shown on **Worksheet 1.5 (p. 22)**, then write a sentence summarizing what you see as God's purpose in human affairs.

Leader Notes

Divide the class into two or more sections. Assign those in each section one or more selected verses from the list on Worksheet 1.5. Allow three or four minutes for people to read and then write a brief statement of God's purpose as revealed in Scripture. Invite volunteers to read their statements aloud.

A Guidebook. In light of God's stated purpose to create a people who honor him, it is no surprise to discover that the intended purpose of the Bible is to guide us to love and obey God. Every time the Bible makes reference to God communicating to people, either through written or spoken messages, it is always either clearly stated or obviously implied that God expects the recipients of the message to do something as a result. It is never his intention that anyone would simply listen or read in order to acquire interesting knowledge. Ultimately, the Bible is not a book of history, or poetry, or prophecy, or correspondence. It is a guidebook to be read and put into practice.

"Do not merely listen to the word, and so deceive yourselves. Do what it says. Anyone who listens to the word but does not do what it says is like a man who looks at his face in a mirror and, after looking at himself, goes away and immediately forgets what he looks like. But the man who looks intently into the perfect law that gives freedom, and continues to do this, not forgetting what he has heard, but doing it—he will be blessed in what he does." James 1:22-25

> Instruct people to work together in groups of no more than four or five people to write a descriptive comparison of reading the Bible but not applying what was read.

❑ Complete this statement using a different analogy than the one James used:

Reading or studying the Bible without putting into practice what it teaches is like...

_____

_____

10 MINUTES **Step 4:   Where Do I Start?—
Choosing What to Study First**

Pray About Your Bible Reading Plans.   Take time to talk to God about how he can talk to you through his Word. Be open and honest with him about any barriers you may be facing (crowded schedule, limited Bible knowledge, lack of discipline, personal doubts, etc.). Ask for his guidance and help as you seek to learn more about him through his Word.

Become Part of a Bible Study Group.   Most people find that group study provides a great deal of help in pursuing personal Bible study. Even if the group is not currently focusing on the area of your greatest interest, the support and encouragement of a group can make it well worth your while to postpone your own individualized reading goals for a while.

- Find out what Bible study options are available through your church, then get involved with one.
- Talk to the leader or others in the group for tips on Bible passages to read between group meetings.
- If your pastor is presenting a sermon series, find out what passages you could read that parallel each week's topic.

Share an experience of how a group Bible study (Sunday morning, electives, home study group, etc.) has been helpful to you. Suggest opportunities for group study that will be available in the coming months.

Set Aside Time for Bible Reading and Prayer. You are not likely to *find* time in the middle of a busy schedule to pick up your Bible and start reading. You need to look at your calendar and *set aside* time. For many people, scheduling the same time period each day works best, thereby building Bible reading into their daily routine. Others find it works better for them to schedule different time periods depending on each day's activities. The important thing is to be realistic and consistent.

Share your own plan for Bible reading and prayer. Be honest about any difficulties you encounter in following through with it. Briefly tell why Bible reading and prayer are important in your life.

Define a Bible Reading Plan You Can Follow. Avoid the temptation to start with plans you may not be able to carry out. Start with brief, simple passages, then gradually work your way to longer, more challenging parts of Scripture. It is better to read, think about, understand, and apply just one verse, than to "cover" chapters without putting truth into practice. "A One-Month Introduction to Your Bible" in *The Bible: Easy Access Guide* booklet is a good plan for getting started.

Focus on Today, Not on the Past. Whatever part of Scripture you study, knowing the original setting and purpose of a Bible book is important. However, historical knowledge is not the ultimate goal. The true purpose of God's Word has always been to guide us in how we live our lives. Here are a few tips to help.

Gain Benefit from What You Read

Select one of these tips listed on the next page that has been beneficial in your Bible study. Describe how following that suggestion has been helpful to you.

- Pray before and after you read. The Bible is God's Word, so ask him for help to understand and apply it.
- Read any passages both before and after a group study. You get more out of the group meeting if you read the passages first, and you get more out of the passages if you read them again afterward.
- In reading stories from the Bible, look for what you can learn from both positive and negative examples.
- When reading the words of Jesus or New Testament letters, imagine the words being spoken to you. Mentally insert your own name in some of the verses. For example, "For God so loved [Mike] that he gave his one and only Son, that [Mike] believes in him...." (John 3:16).
- Pause during and after reading to answer these three questions about what you have read: What does it mean? What does it mean to me? What do I need to do about it?

10–15 MINUTES INTO LIFE

Benefits the Bible Brings

Psalm 119 is the longest chapter in the Bible. It is a magnificent poem extolling God's Word. It is divided into twenty-two stanzas, the verses of each one beginning with a different letter of the Hebrew alphabet.

Leader Notes

> Divide the class into groups of no more than four or five per group. Assign each group a different stanza of Psalm 119, and ask them to list the benefits from heeding God's Word. Then, ask a member from each group to share the group's list with the others.

❏ Choose one stanza from Psalm 119. List the benefits mentioned there of reading and obeying God's Word.

_____

_____

_____

_____

Leader Notes

Have each person choose and share one benefit from their group's list. Then have group members pray for each other.

❑ Choose one of the benefits listed. Pray for God's help in experiencing and enjoying that benefit as you study the Bible in the coming weeks.

❑ Pull out the booklet, _The Bible: Easy Access Guide._ Keep it with your Bible as a helpful summary of key points covered in this course.

❑ Begin a Bible study plan, such as "A One-Month Introduction to Your Bible" in the _Easy Access Guide._

WORKSHEET 1.1

Read the following declarations, then write a reason why each one is a significant reason to study the Bible.

THE BIBLE IS...	I SHOULD STUDY IT BECAUSE...
"Your word, O LORD, is eternal; it stands firm in the heavens." Psalm 119:89	
"How sweet are your words to my taste, sweeter than honey to my mouth!" Psalm 119:103	
"Your word is a lamp to my feet and a light for my path." Psalm 119:105	
"The grass withers and the flowers fall, but the word of our God stands forever." Isaiah 40:8	
"For the word of God is living and active. Sharper than any double-edged sword, it penetrates even to dividing soul and spirit, joints and marrow; it judges the thoughts and attitudes of the heart." Hebrews 4:12	
"For you have been born again, not of perishable seed, but of imperishable, through the living and enduring word of God." 1 Peter 1:23	

WORKSHEET 1.2

Select two quotations from the list below that you find most persuasive in encouraging you to study the Bible. Write a statement telling why these quotations appeal to you.

"There is no book like the Bible for excellent wisdom and use." *Sir Matthew Hale, seventeenth century English jurist*

"There never was found, in any age of the world, either religion or law that did so highly exalt the public good as the Bible." *Francis Bacon, sixteenth century English scientist and philosopher*

"It is a belief in the Bible, the fruit of deep meditation, which has served me as the guide of my moral and literary life." *Johan Wolfgang von Goethe, seventeenth century German poet and philosopher*

"When you have read the Bible, you will know it is the word of God, because you will have found it the key to your own heart, your own happiness and your own duty." *Woodrow Wilson, twenty-eighth president of the United States*

"I find more sure marks of authenticity in the Bible than in any profane history whatever." *Isaac Newton, seventeenth century English scientist*

"Nobody ever outgrows Scripture; the book widens and deepens with our years." *Charles Spurgeon, nineteenth century English preacher*

"Americans need to read the Bible. Even more, they need to study it. It is the cornerstone of freedom, the foundation of idealism, and the modus operandi of abundant living." *Billy Graham, twentieth century evangelist*

_____

_____

_____

WORKSHEET 1.3

Consider each of the following affirmations about the continuing value of God's Word. Then, alongside each verse, write one or more current issues that that verse calls to your mind as something Scripture effectively addresses.

GOD'S WORD	
YESTERDAY'S PROMISE	**TODAY'S CONCERNS**
"But the LORD said to Samuel… "The LORD does not look at the things man looks at. Man looks at the outward appearance, but the LORD looks at the heart." 1 Samuel 16:7	
"Search me, O God, and know my heart; test me and know my anxious thoughts. See if there is any offensive way in me, and lead me in the way everlasting." Psalm 139:23, 24	
"Heaven and earth will pass away, but my words will never pass away." Matthew 24:35	
"But these are written that you may believe that Jesus is the Christ, the Son of God, and that by believing you may have life in his name." John 20:31	
"These things happened to them (Israelites) as examples and were written down as warnings for us, on whom the fulfillment of the ages has come. So, if you think you are standing firm, be careful that you don't fall!" 1 Corinthians 10:11, 12	
"His (God's) intent was that now, through the church, the manifold wisdom of God should be made known to the rulers and authorities in the heavenly realms, according to his eternal purpose which he accomplished in Christ Jesus our Lord." Ephesians 3:10, 11	
"Remember your leaders, who spoke the word of God to you. Consider the outcome of their way of life and imitate their faith. Jesus Christ is the same yesterday and today and forever." Hebrews 13:7, 8	

WORKSHEET 1.4

On the following charts, match the names of at least five of the characters to the books in which their stories are found. The references listed alongside some of the books are clues that mention the characters in the list.

THE BIBLE: A UNIQUE LIBRARY
OLD TESTAMENT (39 BOOKS—BEFORE JESUS)

Match the books and references to the characters.

BOOKS AND REFERENCES		CHARACTERS TO MATCH
History (17)	**Prophecy (17)**	Rahab
The Law:	*Major Prophets:*	Esther
Genesis (6:9; 21:1, 2;	Isaiah	Jacob and Esau
25:34; 37:3)	Jeremiah	Saul
Exodus (4:19)	Lamentations	Naomi
Leviticus	Ezekiel	David
Numbers	Daniel	Abraham and Sarah
Deuteronomy	*Minor Prophets:*	Elijah
History:	Hosea	Gideon
Joshua (6:25)	Joel	Hezekiah
Judges (4:4; 6:11; 13:24)	Amos	Joseph
Ruth (1:22)	Obadiah	Samuel
1 Samuel (3:1; 10:1; 16:13)	Jonah	Ezra
2 Samuel	Micah	Noah
1 Kings (2:1; 17:1)	Nahum	Deborah
2 Kings (18:1)	Habakkuk	Solomon
1 Chronicles	Zephaniah	Samson
2 Chronicles	Haggai	Moses
Ezra (7:8)	Zechariah	
Nehemiah	Malachi	
Esther (4:12)		
Poetry (5)		
Job		
Psalms		
Proverbs		
Ecclesiastes		
Song of Solomon		

continued

THE BIBLE: A UNIQUE LIBRARY
NEW TESTAMENT (27 BOOKS—JESUS AND THE CHURCH)

Match the books and references to the characters.

BOOKS AND REFERENCES	CHARACTERS TO MATCH
History (5) *The Gospels:* 　Matthew (1:18; 4:18) 　Mark (1:4) 　Luke (10:38, 39) 　John (20:24) *History:* 　Acts (9:1) **Letters (21)** *To Churches:* 　Romans 　1, 2 Corinthians 　Galatians 　Ephesians 　Philippians 　Colossians 　1, 2 Thessalonians *To Individuals:* 　1, 2 Timothy 　Titus 　Philemon *General Letters:* 　Hebrews 　James 　1, 2 Peter 　1, 2, 3 John 　Jude **Prophecy (1)** 　Revelation	Peter Paul (Saul) Mary and Martha Mary John the Baptist Thomas

WORKSHEET 1.5

Read the following verses, then write a sentence summarizing what you see as God's purpose in human affairs.

SCRIPTURE	GOD'S PURPOSE
"Know therefore that the LORD your God is God; he is the faithful God, keeping his covenant of love to a thousand generations of those who love him and keep his commands." Deuteronomy 7:9	
"Turn to me and be saved, all you ends of the earth; for I am God, and there is no other." Isaiah 45:22	
"I make known the end from the beginning, from ancient times, what is still to come. I say: My purpose will stand, and I will do all that I please.... I am bringing my righteousness near, it is not far away; and my salvation will not be delayed. I will grant salvation to Zion, my splendor to Israel." Isaiah 46:10, 13	
"For my Father's will is that everyone who looks to the Son and believes in him shall have eternal life." John 6:40	
"This man (Jesus) was handed over to you by God's set purpose and foreknowledge; and you... put him to death by nailing him to the cross." Acts 2:23	
"His intent was that now, through the church, the manifold wisdom of God should be made known to the rulers and authorities in the heavenly realms, according to his eternal purpose which he accomplished in Christ Jesus our Lord." Ephesians 3:10, 11	

LESSON 2

The Books of History

"Bible stories are for kids," the man said. "You know, like in those big picture books."

"But what about all the violence and sex in a lot of Bible stories?" the other man asked. "Those don't seem much like kid stories to me."

This conversation illustrates the ambivalent feelings many people have toward the Old Testament books of history. On one hand, many of the stories have been favorites of many generations of children (e.g., Moses in the bullrushes, David and Goliath, Jonah and the whale, Daniel in the lion's den). On the other hand, the stories deal with very adult themes (e.g., Abraham and Hagar, David and Bathsheba). And all the narratives have meanings and insights beyond the interest or understanding of children, giving a richness and depth that challenge any adult. The Bible is primarily an adult book—about adults, by adults, for adults. The many familiar and unfamiliar stories contained in the seventeen books of Old Testament history are full of examples, truths, and instructions of great value for all adults.

LESSON 2—THE BOOKS OF HISTORY

OUTLINE

- Patriarchs and Promises
- Founding of the Nation
- Kings and Prophets
- Exile and Return

LEARNING ACTIVITIES

❑ Throughout this lesson you will find a variety of helpful learning activities indicated by a check box ❑. Mark the check box when you complete each activity.

LESSON TIME: 60–75 minutes

 10–15 MINUTES

INTO THE LESSON

I've Heard of You

Many Bible names are very familiar and continue to be popular centuries later. People still give boys names such as Adam, David, Jonathan, Samuel, or Joseph. And little girls are still called Sarah, Ruth, Rebekah, Miriam, or Esther. The same cannot be said of all Bible names, however. Some are avoided because of the loathsome character of the original bearer: Jezebel or Absalom. Others are probably too odd-sounding for most people's taste: Mephibosheth, Zerubbabel, or Jehosheba.

Leader Notes

As participants arrive, divide them into two or more small groups or teams to work together in identifying the twenty Bible characters in the list on Worksheet 2.1. Once a group believes they have identified all twenty characters, call for volunteers to tell which description matches which character.

❑ Test your recollection of some of the most famous names from the Old Testament books of history. Using

Worksheet 2.1 (p. 37), match the names with the descriptions of the characters. Write the character's name in front of the appropriate description. (NOTE: You may look up any of these references to check your answers. [All the references are for books near the front of the Bible, except for Acts, which is in the New Testament, toward the back.] Correct answers are printed at the end of the lesson.)

40–45 MINUTES INTO THE WORD

"And what more shall I say? I do not have time to tell about Gideon, Barak, Samson, Jephthah, David, Samuel and the prophets, who through faith conquered kingdoms, administered justice, and gained what was promised; who shut the mouths of lions, quenched the fury of the flames, and escaped the edge of the sword; whose weakness was turned to strength; and who became powerful in battle and routed foreign armies." Hebrews 11:32-34

Should anyone think the narratives in the books of history have little to say to people today, one reading of Hebrews 11 should dispel that notion. The books of history are filled with stories of God's dealings with real people and their struggles, defeats, and victories. Truly, there is much excitement, adventure, and practical instruction in these pages. This lesson presents an overview of the books of history and gives you an opportunity to study a Bible character. We can learn a great deal by focusing on God's interaction with a specific person.

15 MINUTES Step 1: Patriarchs and Promises

Leader Notes

> Briefly introduce the book of Genesis and the six major individuals/families it presents. (See list on page 26.) Divide people into pairs or trios and assign each small group one of the six families. Have them look at the selected reference and agree on a statement of an important truth they see in the incident described. After several minutes, invite volunteers to share the truth they identified.

The book of **Genesis** means "beginnings." Not only do we see the beginning of the world we inhabit, but we also see the beginning of God's revelation of himself to humanity. The dominant themes of this opening book are the power, uniqueness, and glory of God; the fallen nature of humanity; and the remedy for sin's consequences—obedient worship of God.

In Genesis we see the first of the covenants that God offered. God agreed to protect and bless those who obey him. Covenants were made with Noah and then Abraham, and repeated to his descendants Isaac and Jacob.

Genesis records the overlapping stories of God's interaction with six individuals and their families, leading us from the Garden of Eden to Pharaoh's palace in Egypt. These narratives have long captured the interest of Bible readers because of their powerful human dramas and the insights they give into the character and attributes of God.

❏ Select one of the six main individuals/families in Genesis. Then look at the selected reference and write a brief statement of an important truth you see in that incident.

MAIN CHARACTERS IN GENESIS	ONE OR TWO IMPORTANT TRUTHS	SELECTED REFERENCE(S)
Adam and Eve (Genesis 1:26–5:5)		Genesis 2:18-25 Genesis 3:1-7
Noah and his family (Genesis 5:28–10:32)		Genesis 8:15-22
Abraham and Sarah (Genesis 11:26–25:11)		Genesis 15:1-6
Isaac and Rebekah (Genesis 21:1-7; 22; 24:1–28:9; 35:27-29)		Genesis 21:1-7 Genesis 24:10-14
Jacob and Rachel (Genesis 25:19-35; 27:1–49:33)		Genesis 28:16-22
Joseph and his brothers (Genesis 37–50)		Genesis 50:15-21

The book of **Exodus** picks up the story of God's people, who were now called Israelites, a long time after the death of Joseph. During that time, the descendants of Abraham, Isaac, and Jacob multiplied greatly. A change in dynasties in Egypt turned the status of the Israelites from that of favored guests to feared and oppressed slaves. God prepared and then called Moses to lead his people out of bondage in Egypt, back to the land he had promised Abraham. Exodus tells of the people's conflict with Egypt's king (Pharaoh), their dramatic escape through the Red Sea, the giving of the Law at Mt. Sinai, and the building of the tabernacle. The books of **Leviticus**, **Numbers**, and **Deuteronomy** continue the story of the years of wandering in the desert, along with the detailed regulations that shaped the unique spiritual life and identity of the chosen people.

A major theme developed through the first five books (the Hebrew Torah) was that the Jews were to be a special people, separated from all that would defile them. The many laws recorded in these books (including the Ten Commandments) provided a complete canon of sacred and civil law for the emerging nation. Religious observances were vitally important, but equally so was a high standard of public and private morality. Because God is a god of justice, all sin and injustice is seen as an offense against him; but repentance always brings forgiveness.

❏ Choose one of the quotations from Moses listed on **Worksheet 2.2 (p. 39)**. Then write a sentence telling why that quote has significance in your life today.

5 MINUTES **Step 2: Founding of the Nation**

Leader Notes

> Have people continue working in the same pairs or trios as before. Have them choose a character from the chart on the next page, read the verses about that person, and write the personal quality they see that they would like to have in their own lives.

Heroes and heroines! The books of **Joshua**, **Judges**, and **Ruth** are filled with them. Men and women who contributed greatly to the gradual and often inconsistent transformation of the Israelites from a weak, divided mob into a nation to be reckoned with. And at all times, even when great numbers of the people were in open rebellion against God, we see his powerful hand at work. First we see Joshua, taking over from Moses, leading the conquest of Canaan, both to claim the Israelites' promised inheritance and to visit God's judgment on the wickedness of the land's inhabitants (Leviticus 18:24-28; Deuteronomy 9:4, 5). Following Joshua, for more than 200 years, God chose leaders, called judges (Judges 2:16) to rescue his people from enemy oppression and the people's own tendency to reject God and his ways. Repeatedly we see examples of God's justice as he punished both Israelites and Canaanites who had done evil. And just as frequently we see demonstrations of God's merciful forgiveness as he provided opportunity after opportunity for people to return to his ways.

❏ Choose a character from the chart below. Use the Divide and Locate method explained on page 29 to locate the reference for that character. Read the verses about that person, and write the personal quality you see that you would like to have in your own life.

CHARACTER	REFERENCE	QUALITY
Joshua	Joshua 1:6-9	
Rahab	Joshua 6:24, 25	
Caleb	Joshua 14:13, 14	
Deborah	Judges 4:4-9	
Gideon	Judges 6:11-14	
Ruth	Ruth 1:14-18	

Divide and Locate: Another Way to Find Bible References

Besides using the contents page of the Bible to locate references, there is a quick way to open the Bible at or near the reference you want to find. When looking for one of the seventeen Old Testament books of history, either start from the front to get to one of the five books of the law (Genesis, Exodus, Leviticus, Numbers, or Deuteronomy), or try dividing the first quarter of the Bible's pages from those that follow. You will find yourself near the end of the books of history, which in most Bibles is probably in 1 or 2 Samuel. (Obviously, a Bible with many introductory pages will skew this procedure slightly.) From the books of Samuel, you can quickly go back a few pages into Ruth, Judges, or Joshua. Or, flip ahead into the books of Kings or Chronicles.

10–15 MINUTES Step 3: Kings and Prophets

Leader Notes

Briefly introduce people to the books of Samuel, Kings, and Chronicles. Then read the description of King Josiah from 2 Kings 23:25. Ask a volunteer to read aloud the passage about Josiah from 2 Chronicles 34:29-33. Invite volunteers to share their answers to the two questions about Josiah listed on page 31.

Six Old Testament books cover the more than 400 years when Israel was ruled by kings: **1** and **2 Samuel, 1** and **2 Kings,** and **1** and **2 Chronicles.** (Each of these three pairs of books were originally single books. They were each divided in half when the Old Testament was translated into Greek, probably because it was easier to use two smaller scrolls than one very large one.) The books of Samuel and Kings tell a continuous story. The books of Chronicles retell, sometimes with more detail, many of the same events from 2 Samuel and 1 and 2 Kings. Chronicles focuses on the history of Judah, the southern kingdom, which survived more than 100 years after Israel, the northern kingdom, was taken captive by Assyria (721 B.C.). The following chart shows how the books of Chronicles overlap the books of Samuel and Kings:

1 Samuel	2 Samuel	1 Kings	2 Kings
	1 Chronicles	2 Chronicles	

These major events and characters are recounted in these six books:

MAIN PERIODS	MAJOR CHARACTERS	WHO THEY WERE	REFERENCE(S)
Transition from theocracy to monarchy	Samuel	last of the judges and one of the greatest prophets	1 Samuel 1–9
"Golden Age" of Israel's monarchy	Saul, David, Solomon	Israel's first kings	1 Samuel 10– 1 Kings 11; 1 Chronicles 10– 2 Chronicles 9
Division of the kingdom	Ahab, *Asa, Azariah (Uzziah), Jehoshaphat*, Jehu, *Joash* Elijah, Elisha	major kings of *Judah (southern kingdom)* and Israel (northern kingdom); prophets	1 Kings 12– 2 Kings 16; 2 Chronicles 10–28
Fall of Israel and Judah	*Hezekiah, Manasseh, Josiah* Isaiah, Jeremiah	last three major kings of *Judah* prophets	2 Kings 17–25; 2 Chronicles 29-36

The narrative often becomes complex as these six books touch on the lives of scores of leaders in two divergent kingdoms, yet again and again we are reminded of God's covenant with his people. Each king's rule is summarized, not with a list of political, military, or economic achievements, but in terms of obedience to God's laws. The role of the prophets is repeatedly portrayed as the voice of God, calling both king and people to live up to the provisions of the covenant relationship.

❏ Read 2 Chronicles 34:29-33, a brief description of the reign of Josiah, the last great king of Judah. (2 Kings 23:25 says of Josiah, "Neither before nor after Josiah was there a king like him who turned to the LORD as he did—with all his heart and with all his soul and with all his strength, in accordance with all the Law of Moses.") Then answer these questions:

1. What role did God's Word play in Josiah's life?

_____

_____

2. What was the result of Josiah's reading God's Word?

_____

_____

10 MINUTES   **Step 4: Exile and Return**

Leader Notes

Briefly introduce people to the books of Ezra, Nehemiah, and Esther. Then have everyone find Ezra 8. Read aloud the first ten verses, then guide the group in responding to the questions that start on page 33.

Much of what we know about the trauma of Jerusalem's fall and the captivity of its people is based on writings of the prophets Jeremiah, Daniel, Ezekiel, and Obadiah. Then three brief but important books of history give us a look at the struggles involved in returning from exile, and the tenuous but special status of the Jews who lived far from their homeland.

In the earliest Hebrew manuscripts, the books of **Ezra** and **Nehemiah** appear as one book. The narrative is continuous, telling of the stages of the return from exile in Babylon, the rebuilding of the temple (a much humbler one than the one Solomon built), the rebuilding of Jerusalem's walls, the reading of the Law, and the reestablishment of godly worship and holy living. After centuries of flirting and then embracing the idolatry and immorality of other nations, the years of exile combined with the godly leadership of Zerubbabel, Haggai, Zechariah, Ezra, and Nehemiah made a lasting impact on the people. Worship of idols was never again a major problem among the Jews.

The book of **Esther** tells of a young Jewish exile who became queen of Persia, then used her position of influence to save her people from a vicious plot to destroy them. This is the only book in the Bible that makes no direct reference to God, prayer, or any religious observance. But God's protective hand is clearly seen in the details of this suspenseful story.

These final books of Old Testament history powerfully emphasize God's continuing faithfulness to his people. His faithfulness is shown both in his loving reception of all who return to him, and in his judgment on those who persist in doing evil. Clearly, God had formed a nation that recognized his unique superiority, a vital foundation in preparing the way for the coming of the long-promised Messiah.

CHRONOLOGY OF EXILE AND RETURN			
EVENT	MAIN CHARACTERS	DATE	REFERENCE(S)
First deportation	Nebuchadnezzar, king of Babylon; Jehoiakim, king of Judah; Jeremiah, prophet	605 B.C.	2 Kings 24; 2 Chronicles 36
Fall of Jerusalem	Nebuchadnezzar; Zedekiah, king of Judah; Jeremiah	586 B.C.	2 Kings 25; 2 Chronicles 36
First exiles return	Cyrus, king of Persia; Zerubbabel, Jewish leader	538 B.C.	Ezra 1, 2
Temple rebuilding completed	Darius, king of Persia; Zerubbabel; Haggai and Zechariah, prophets	516 B.C.	Ezra 6
Additional exiles return	Artaxerxes, king of Persia; Ezra, priest and scribe	458 B.C.	Ezra 7
Jerusalem wall rebuilt	Artaxerxes; Nehemiah, Jewish cupbearer to the king	445 B.C.	Nehemiah 1–6

❏ Find and read Nehemiah 8:1-10, the account of Ezra reading God's Word to the crowd of returned exiles.

(Again, practice dividing off the first quarter of the Bible, then flip ahead until you come to Nehemiah.) Then answer these questions:

1. What evidence do you see in this passage that the people considered this reading of God's Word to be important to them?

   _____

   _____

2. In addition to reading, the Levites were responsible for "making it clear and giving the meaning so that the people could understand what was being read." Why was that important?

   _____

   _____

3. The reading of the Word resulted in the people weeping with remorse as they learned how far short they had fallen of obeying God. Why do you suppose Nehemiah and Ezra told the people to celebrate instead of weep? (See verse 12.)

   _____

   _____

4. What was the next step in the people's response to God's Word? (See chapter 9, verses 1-3.)

   _____

   _____

10–15 MINUTES **INTO LIFE**

Lead the class in finding Genesis 26:12-33. Read aloud the story of Isaac and the wells. Then divide the class into groups of no more than four or five per group. Instruct the groups to discuss the questions below. If time permits, invite volunteers to share responses to the questions. Then close in prayer.

One of the easiest and most practical ways to study the Bible and gain insights for personal application is to read a complete story and compare the characters' actions with your own in similar situations. The examples of others, both good and bad, are highly instructive. ("These things happened to them as examples and were written down as warnings for us." 1 Corinthians 10:11)

❏ Find and read Genesis 26:12-33, the story about Isaac's efforts to find water for his herds. Then answer the questions that follow the notes below. Take time to pray, asking to learn about yourself and about God from Isaac's example.

NOTES:

26:12—"that land"—Gerar, at the south of Palestine, part of the land God had promised Abraham and Isaac

26:16—Abimelech—king of the Philistines

26:20—Esek—"dispute"

26:21—Sitnah—"opposition"

26:22—Rehoboth—"room"

26:33—Shibah—"seven" or "oath";
Beersheba—"well of the oath" or "seventh well"

1. Knowing that God had promised this land to him, why do you think Isaac did not press his claim and defend his wells against the Philistines?

_____

_____

2. How would the outcome have been different if Isaac had fought for his wells?

_____

_____

3. How do you usually react when threatened with the loss of something that is rightfully yours?

_____

_____

4. To what extent does a tendency to quarrel block us from experiencing God's presence in difficult situations?

_____

_____

5. What actions can you take that will remind you to follow Isaac's example of seeking peace rather than confrontation?

_____

_____

Answers to "I've Heard of You" Quiz:

Gideon; Eve; Joseph; Hezekiah; Moses; Nehemiah; Samson; Abram; Rahab; Elijah; Samuel; David; Zerubbabel; Naomi; Deborah; Solomon; Ezra; Esther; Saul; Jacob

WORKSHEET 2.1

Test your recollection of some of the most famous names from the Old Testament books of history. Match the names with the descriptions of the characters. Write the character's name in front of the appropriate description. (NOTE: You may look up any of these references to check your answers. [All the references are for books near the front of the Bible, except for Acts, which is in the New Testament, toward the back.])

I'VE HEARD OF YOU			
Abram	Eve	Joseph	Samson
David	Ezra	Moses	Samuel
Deborah	Gideon	Naomi	Saul
Elijah	Hezekiah	Nehemiah	Solomon
Esther	Jacob	Rahab	Zerubbabel

NAME	DESCRIPTION	REFERENCE(S)
	Judge who led army of three hundred in victory over Midian	Judges 6–8
	First woman, created as companion for Adam	Genesis 1, 2
	Son of Jacob, sold into slavery, became administrator of Egypt	Genesis 37–50
	King, led people to withstand siege of Jerusalem by Assyria	2 Kings 18–20 2 Chronicles 29–32
	Raised in Pharaoh's house, led Israel's exodus from slavery	Exodus–Deuteronomy
	Rebuilt walls of Jerusalem after captivity	Nehemiah 1–7
	Judge with great strength, betrayed by pride and his lover	Judges 13–16
	Original name of Abraham, "father" of Hebrew nation	Genesis 11:26–25:11
	Harlot who protected Israel's spies in Jericho	Joshua 2, 6

continued

I'VE HEARD OF YOU			
Abram	Eve	Joseph	Samson
David	Ezra	Moses	Samuel
Deborah	Gideon	Naomi	Saul
Elijah	Hezekiah	Nehemiah	Solomon
Esther	Jacob	Rahab	Zerubbabel

NAME	DESCRIPTION	REFERENCE(S)
	Prophet who confronted King Ahab and prophets of Baal	1 Kings 17–19
	Last and greatest judge, first prophet, anointed first kings	1 Samuel 3–16
	King, warrior, poet, musician, "a man after [God's] own heart"	1 Samuel 16– 1 Kings 2; Acts 13:22
	Led initial rebuilding of temple after captivity	Ezra 1–4
	Mother-in-law of Ruth	Ruth 1–4
	Judge and prophet, led victory against chariots of Canaan	Judges 4–5
	King, David's son, built temple, known for great wisdom	1 Kings 2–11
	Scribe who led reforms upon return from captivity	Ezra 7–10
	Queen who risked herself to save her people from slaughter	Esther 1–9
	First king of Israel	1 Samuel 9–31
	Son of Isaac, father of twelve sons who founded Israel's tribes	Genesis 25:19–49:33

WORKSHEET 2.2

Choose one of the following quotations from Moses. Then, in the space below, write a sentence telling why that quote has significance in your life today.

A Few Quotes from Moses

❏ "Hear, O Israel: The LORD our God, the LORD is one. Love the LORD your God with all your heart and with all your soul and with all your strength." Deuteronomy 6:4, 5

❏ "Know therefore that the LORD your God is God; he is the faithful God, keeping his covenant of love to a thousand generations of those who love him and keep his commands." Deuteronomy 7:9

❏ "And now, O Israel, what does the LORD your God ask of you but to fear the LORD your God, to walk in all his ways, to love him, to serve the LORD your God with all your heart and with all your soul, and to observe the LORD's commands and decrees that I am giving you today for your own good?" Deuteronomy 10:12, 13

❏ "Now what I am commanding you today is not too difficult for you or beyond your reach. It is not up in heaven, so that you have to ask, 'Who will ascend into heaven to get it and proclaim it to us so we may obey it?' Nor is it beyond the sea, so that you have to ask, 'Who will cross the sea to get it and proclaim it to us so we may obey it?' No, the word is very near you; it is in your mouth and in your heart so you may obey it." Deuteronomy 30:11-14

❏ "I will proclaim the name of the LORD. Oh, praise the greatness of our God! He is the Rock, his works are perfect, and all his ways are just. A faithful God who does no wrong, upright and just is he." Deuteronomy 32:3, 4

Why Moses' words are significant in my life today:

_____

_____

_____

_____

LESSON 3

The Poets and Prophets

A young boy thumbed carefully through his grandmother's well-worn Bible. He noticed many places where she had underlined text and others where she had added notes in the margins. Then he turned the Bible and stared at the edges of the pages.

"Grandma," he asked. "Why are the edges of some pages all shiny but others aren't?"

Grandma looked at the pages her grandson indicated. "I guess," she answered, "it's because I've read those pages a lot more than I have the ones that are still shiny."

"Why's that?" the boy asked.

Now Grandma looked more closely at those well-worn pages. Then she said, "I guess I've always loved to read the Psalms and Proverbs. But the prophets are a lot harder to understand. So I haven't read them as much."

Grandma's pattern of Bible reading is typical of many other people's experience. Psalms and Proverbs, two of the five books of poetry, are probably the most frequently read Old Testament books. And most of the seventeen prophetic books are read infrequently, in spite of the fact that they contain some of the most uplifting and challenging passages of all books in the Bible.

LESSON 3—THE POETS AND PROPHETS

OUTLINE

- The Books of Poetry
- The Major Prophets
- The Minor Prophets

LEARNING ACTIVITIES

❑ Throughout this lesson you will find a variety of helpful learning activities indicated by a check box ❑. Mark the check box when you complete each activity.

LESSON TIME: 60–75 minutes

10–15 MINUTES

INTO THE LESSON

Puzzling Names

The first challenge you will face when you read the Old Testament poets and prophets is pronouncing the unfamiliar names of these twenty-two books. The list starts out deceptively simple: a book with a three-letter title. The problem here is that "Job" does not refer to a person's work (jawb), but a person's name (jobe). Next comes Psalms, with a silent *P*. Proverbs is easy, but it's followed by Ecclesiastes, an unusual title from a Greek word for teacher. The last book of poetry is titled Song of Songs in some Bibles, Song of Solomon in others, and Canticles (Latin for song) in others.

If those titles do not seem intimidating, scan the seventeen books named after prophets, men with names like Habakkuk, Zephaniah, and Zechariah.

Leader Notes

As participants arrive, invite them to work together in pairs or trios to solve the crossword puzzle on Worksheet 3.1 with the names of the books of poetry and prophecy. Once a group believes they have solved the puzzle, call for volunteers to tell which description matches which character.

❏ To build your familiarity with the names of the books of poetry and prophecy, complete the crossword puzzle on **Worksheet 3.1 (p. 53)**, fitting in the names of each of the twenty-two books. Some clues almost give away the answer. Others might make you think. You might want to have your Bible open to its contents page as you work. The correct answers are printed at the end of the lesson.

40–45 MINUTES # INTO THE WORD

> "Jesus said to them, 'This is what I told you while I was still with you: Everything must be fulfilled that is written about me in the Law of Moses, the Prophets and the Psalms.' Then he opened their minds so they could understand the Scriptures. He told them, 'This is what is written: The Christ will suffer and rise from the dead on the third day, and repentance and forgiveness of sins will be preached in his name to all nations, beginning at Jerusalem.'" Luke 24:44-47

Jesus frequently referred to the Old Testament books of poetry and prophecy. Often he did so because he was quoting predictions of his own life and ministry. The strong links between Christ and the poetic and prophetic books are among the strongest reasons Christians can benefit from reading these parts of Scripture. This lesson presents an overview of the books of poetry and prophecy, and gives you an opportunity to compare selected passages, an approach to Bible study that lets you use Scripture itself to sharpen your understanding of its meaning.

15–20 MINUTES ## Step 1: The Books of Poetry

Leader Notes

> Briefly introduce the five books of poetry.

The five books of poetry express the hopes, fears, laments, thanksgivings, and even the doubts of the Hebrews. The book of **Job**, which contains some of the finest poetry in the Bible, explores the problems of suffering and of human standing before God. The lengthy dialogue between Job and his three friends is a wrenching examination of the popular belief in reward and punishment, concluding that God's purposes are not limited by our actions and understandings.

Many of the **Psalms** were composed for temple worship, while others are intensely personal works of devotion. Many are credited to David, but some came from earlier periods, and some from later periods. **Proverbs** comprises several collections of ancient wisdom. The final form of the book is attributed to Solomon as evidence of his superior wisdom. Solomon also seems responsible for **Ecclesiastes** (Ecclesiastes 1:1), a book that approaches skepticism, but concludes with more traditional wisdom. The **Song of Songs** is a collection of love poems, celebrating love as a wondrous gift from God. Some students also see this as an allegory of Christ's love for the church, although the New Testament never quotes from this book.

Leader Notes

Divide people into at least five groups and assign each small group one of the five books of poetry. (If you do not have enough people to form at least five groups, omit assigning one or more of the five books.) Have groups look at the selected passages and discuss what the passages have in common and how they differ. After several minutes, invite volunteers to share one thing they noted as they compared and contrasted the passages.

❑ Compare and contrast two passages from at least one of the books of poetry. Use the Divide and Locate method explained on page 45 to find these verses, then answer the questions that follow.

BOOK	REFERENCE 1	REFERENCE 2
Job	9:1-10	40:1-10
Psalms	23:1-6	91:1-16
Proverbs	4:10-13; 20-27	6:20-23
Ecclesiastes	1:12-18	5:10-20
Song of Songs	2:8-13	4:8-15

Divide and Locate: Another Way to Find Bible References

In the previous lesson you were introduced to a quick way to open the Bible at or near the reference you want to find.

When looking for an Old Testament book of history, either start from the front to locate one of the five books of the law (Genesis, Exodus, Leviticus, Numbers, or Deuteronomy), or divide the first quarter of the Bible's pages from those that follow. In most Bibles you will find yourself in 1 or 2 Samuel.

To find a book of poetry, divide the Bible in half. In most Bibles you will be in Psalms or Proverbs. Turn toward the front to locate Job, or toward the back to move into Ecclesiastes or Song of Songs.

1. What do the two passages have in common?

   _____

   _____

   _____

2. What is different between the two passages?

   _____

   _____

   _____

3. After reading both, what main thoughts stand out to you?

   _____

   _____

   _____

4. If these two passages were all you knew about the books of poetry, what impression would you have about this section of the Old Testament?

_____

_____

_____

15 MINUTES   **Step 2:   The Major Prophets**

Leader Notes

Briefly introduce the books of prophecy.

It is unfortunate that the prophetic books have traditionally been separated into the "major" and "minor" prophets based on the size of the books. This arrangement causes the reader to lose sight of the distinct impact each prophet had on his own time in history. Thus, let's consider the probable order in which the prophets appeared on the scene.

Joel may have been the first of the writing prophets (ninth century B.C.), but some scholars believe he could have been one of the last. In three vivid chapters he compares God's judgment to an invasion of locusts and calls the people to repent.

The prophets of the eighth century B.C. were **Jonah**, **Amos**, **Hosea**, **Isaiah**, and **Micah**. They declared God's holiness and his righteous judgment on the idol worship and moral depravity of both Hebrew kingdoms (Israel and Judah). They called their leaders and people back to the covenant God had made with their ancestors.

Nahum, first of the seventh century B.C. prophets, announced the destruction of Nineveh (621 B.C.), capital of the Assyrian empire. **Zephaniah** and **Habakkuk** belong to the same century and warn Judah of coming judgment at the hands of Babylon. **Jeremiah** was the greatest prophet of the seventh century B.C. He called Judah to turn back to God, he warned the people to not depend on military alliances with foreign nations, and commanded them to not resist the Babylonian invasion, as it was evidence of God's judgment. He also dramatically recorded his own inner spiritual struggles. **Lamentations**, probably written by Jeremiah, reflects the miseries of Jerusalem's destruction and the exile that followed.

During the period of Babylonian exile, **Ezekiel** encouraged the return of the Jews to the Holy Land, promising a glorious restoration of the nation. **Daniel** also promised God's help through times of national and international upheaval. **Obadiah** declared judgment on the Edomites because of their assistance to Babylon in conquering Judah, and their subsequent looting of the defeated city.

The remaining prophets followed the exile. The entire book of **Haggai** and the first eight chapters of **Zechariah** encouraged the rebuilding of a small temple in Jerusalem. **Joel**, the last six chapters of **Zechariah**, and **Malachi** all stress the themes of judgment and restoration.

All the prophets saw Israel (and Judah) as having a special place in God's purpose and love, called to be a light to the nations. The people, and often the prophets as well, struggled to accept the concepts of God's impartial justice, and his love toward Israel and the rest of humanity.

Leader Notes

With people in the same small groups as earlier, assign the following list of declarations of God's restoration of his people. Half of the groups should start from the top of the list, while the others read from the bottom of the list. Instruct people to look for common ideas in the passages they read.

❑ Compare two or more of these passages from the major prophets:

- Isaiah 40:25-31
- Jeremiah 31:15-18
- Lamentations 5:19-21
- Ezekiel 37:1-3, 11-14
- Daniel 9:17-19

Divide and Locate: Another Way to Find Bible References

Continue practicing this quick way to open the Bible at or near the reference you want to find.

When looking for a book of major prophecy, divide the Bible in half. In most Bibles you will be in Psalms or Proverbs. Then turn toward the back to move into Isaiah, Jeremiah, and the others.

1. What do the passages have in common?

_____

_____

_____

2. What is different among the passages?

_____

_____

_____

3. After reading these passages, what main thoughts stand out to you?

_____

_____

_____

4. If these two passages were all you knew about the books of prophecy, what impression would you have about this section of the Old Testament?

_____

_____

_____

10 MINUTES   **Step 3: The Minor Prophets**

Leader Notes

> Refer to Worksheet 3.2. Lead the group in matching the beginning of the verse with the conclusion of the quotes from the minor prophets. Guide them in locating any they are not sure how to match.

❑ Using **Worksheet 3.2 (p. 54)**, match the beginning of the verse with the conclusion of the quotes from the minor prophets.

Divide and Locate: Another Way to Find Bible References

Continue practicing this quick way to open the Bible at or near the reference you want to find.

When looking for a book of minor prophecy, divide the Bible in half, then divide the second half in half again. In most Bibles you will be in Matthew, the first book of the New Testament. Then turn toward the front to move into Malachi, Zechariah, or one of the other minor prophecy books.

Leader Notes

> Have everyone find a partner. Ask each group member to choose one verse from the chart on Worksheet 3.2 to read aloud to his or her partner. Then ask each member to tell his or her partner one reason that verse is meaningful to him or her.

❏ Choose one of the verses from the chart on **Worksheet 3.2 (p. 54)** to read aloud (to another person or to yourself) as a promise worth remembering.

1. I chose the following verse:

_____

_____

2. This verse is meaningful to me because:

_____

_____

_____

10–15 MINUTES INTO LIFE

Leader Notes

> Instruct half the class to locate Micah 6:6-8 while the other half finds Zechariah 7:8-10. Invite a volunteer from each group to read aloud their passage. Then lead the class in answering the questions that compare these passages. Finally, close in prayer.

The Message of the Prophets

These two brief, but similar, passages were written about 200 years apart, but they are powerful summaries of what all the prophets said God wants people to do.

- Micah 6:6-8 (Micah lived during the eighth century B.C., during the reigns of Ahaz and Hezekiah in Judah.)

- Zechariah 7:8-10 (Zechariah lived in Jerusalem after the exile to Babylon, and was a contemporary of Ezra and Nehemiah.)

❏ Read the two passages, then answer the questions on page 51.

1. What do the passages have in common?

   _____

   _____

   _____

2. What is different between the passages?

   _____

   _____

   _____

3. After reading these passages, what main thoughts
   stand out to you?

   _____

   _____

   _____

4. Based on these two passages, what does God consider most important about the way you are living
   your life?

   _____

   _____

   _____

WORKSHEET 3.1

PUZZLING NAMES

ACROSS

4 Z-, but not Zephaniah
7 One of five -iah prophets
8 Formal for "Zeke"
11 Musical title—a love poem
13 Not pronounced "Jawb"
14 Songs with a "P"
17 A BIG fish story
18 He had wife troubles
19 Not just another funny name

DOWN

1 The "teacher"
2 Thrown to the lions
3 Said Bethlehem will produce Messiah
4 Obviously not Zechariah
5 Encouraged temple rebuilding
6 Short, pithy sayings
9 A lot of sadness here
10 First of "major" prophets
12 Nothing HO-hum here
13 The "weeping prophet"
15 The end of the Old Testament
16 A shepherd from Judah
17 One of three J- prophets

WORKSHEET 3.2

Draw a line to connect the start and end of each verse.

MATCH THE START OF EACH VERSE...	...WITH THE CORRECT CONCLUSION
"And afterward, I will pour out my Spirit on all people.	righteousness like a never-failing stream!" Amos 5:24
"I will betroth you to me forever;	Your sons and daughters will prophesy, your old men will dream dreams, your young men will see visions." Joel 2:28
"But let justice roll on like a river,	They will beat their swords into plowshares and their spears into pruning hooks. Nation will not take up sword against nation, nor will they train for war anymore." Micah 4:3
"I knew that you are a gracious and compassionate God, slow to anger and abounding in love,	he makes my feet like the feet of a deer, he enables me to go on the heights." Habakkuk 3:19
"He will judge between many peoples and will settle disputes for strong nations far and wide.	I will betroth you in righteousness and justice, in love and compassion." Hosea 2:19
"The Sovereign LORD is my strength;	He cares for those who trust in him." Nahum 1:7
"The LORD is good, a refuge in times of trouble.	Test me in this,' says the LORD Almighty, 'and see if I will not throw open the flood-gates of heaven and pour out so much blessing that you will not have room enough for it." Malachi 3:10
"The LORD will be king over the whole earth.	He will take great delight in you, he will quiet you with his love, he will rejoice over you with singing." Zephaniah 3:17
"The LORD your God is with you, he is mighty to save.	On that day there will be one LORD, and his name the only name." Zechariah 14:9
"'Bring the whole tithe into the storehouse, that there may be food in my house.	a God who relents from sending calamity." Jonah 4:2

Solution to Puzzling Names Crossword Puzzle:

LESSON 4

The Life of Jesus

After examining the historical evidence for the existence of Jesus and the accuracy of the Gospels, historian Will Durant concluded:

"That a few simple men should in one generation have invented so powerful and appealing a personality, so lofty an ethic and so inspiring a vision of human brotherhood, would be a miracle far more incredible than any recorded in the Gospels. After two centuries of Higher Criticism the outlines of the life, character, and teaching of Christ remain reasonably clear, and constitute the most fascinating feature in the history of Western man." *Will Durant,* The Story of Civilization: Part III: Caesar and Christ. *New York: Simon and Schuster, 1944, p. 557.*

"Close contact with the text of the Gospels builds up in the heart and mind a character of awe-inspiring stature and quality.... These are not embroidered tales; the material is cut to the bone.... No man could ever have invented such a character as Jesus. No man could have set down such artless and vulnerable accounts as these unless some real Event lay behind them." *J. B. Phillips,* The Ring of Truth. *New York: The Macmillan Company, 1967, p. 77.*

While some scholars periodically try to cast doubt on the story presented by Matthew, Mark, Luke, and John, the conclusion stated by Durant and Phillips has been echoed over and over by scholars, students, and ordinary readers. Beyond the vast amounts of evidence supporting the reliability of the texts, the power of these narratives and their depiction of Jesus is remarkably striking, making a lasting impact on everyone who examines these pages.

LESSON 4—THE LIFE OF JESUS

OUTLINE

- The Four Gospels
- Jesus' Birth and Boyhood
- Jesus' Ministry and Teaching
- Jesus' Death and Resurrection

LEARNING ACTIVITIES

❏ Throughout this lesson you will find a variety of helpful learning activities indicated by a check box ❏. Mark the check box when you complete each activity.

LESSON TIME: 60–75 minutes

 10 MINUTES

INTO THE LESSON

Between the Testaments

A person living near the turn of the twenty-first century, if looking back over the preceding 400 years, is likely to be convinced that the world is a vastly different place around the year 2000 than it was in 1600. Similarly, anyone living in Palestine in the year that Jesus was born would view the preceding 400 years as an era of astonishing changes. From the time of Nehemiah, Zechariah, and Malachi, approximately 400 years passed—years filled with political, military, social, and religious upheaval.

Once a powerful nation under the leadership of David and Solomon, Israel and Judah had declined over the centuries. Both nations lost their independent status when they were conquered and enslaved: Israel by Assyria, and then Judah by Babylon. From that time on, even after the return from exile, Israel was only a minor province, controlled by first one then another in a series of powerful empires.

In contrast to the centuries of the judges and kings, however, the influence of these foreign powers did not seduce the Jews into idolatry. The destruction of Jerusalem, the years of exile, and the humiliation of being a subject people accomplished what the warnings of the judges and prophets had not. God's people had finally learned that there is but one true God.

Leader Notes

Before participants arrive, mount two posters on opposite walls of the room: one lettered "End of Old Testament (400 B.C.)"; the other "The New Testament." Stretch a rope or yarn from one sign to the other. At appropriate places on the rope, clip three large index cards: "Alexander the Great, 332 B.C."; "The Maccabean Rebellion, 166 B.C."; and "63 B.C., Rome Conquers Palestine". As people arrive, form them into groups of no more than five or six per group. Assign each group one of the Moments of History to read and discuss the question at the end. After several minutes, invite a volunteer from each group to stand alongside the rope at the approximate position when their assigned "Moment" occurred. Then ask volunteers to share one interesting fact and the group's answer to the question.

❑ Read one or more of these "Moments of History," then answer the question at the end.

The Persians (538–330 B.C.)

Cyrus, king of Persia, issued a decree that paved the way for the return of the captives from Babylon. From that time on, the Persian rulers did not interfere with the Jews' worship of God. Limited political power was allowed the Jews under the direction of the Persian satraps, but religious leadership was the uncontested province of the priests.

The Greeks (330–166 B.C.)

In only a few years' time, Alexander defeated the great Persian Empire and launched a crusade to make the Greek language and culture the unifying forces in human affairs. Following the pattern of the Persians, Alexander and his immediate successors allowed the Jews to continue all their religious observances. However, in 175 B.C., Antiochus IV came to power and attempted to force Greek (Hellenistic) culture and religion on the Jews by destroying all copies of the Torah (Genesis through Deuteronomy) and violating the temple.

The Maccabees (166–63 B.C.)

An elderly priest and his five sons led a revolt against Greek rule. The eldest of the sons, Judas (Maccabeus), took the leadership of a twenty-four-year struggle that finally resulted in independence. Unfortunately, the descendants of these remarkable heroes were fascinated with Greek culture. The resulting aristocratic leadership actually persecuted those who held to orthodox Jewish practice. In the latter years of this dynasty, continuing struggles for supremacy distracted and weakened the nation's leadership.

The Romans (63 B.C.–)

The Roman general Pompey brutally conquered Palestine, breaking a three-month siege of Jerusalem with a massacre of priests in the temple. This desecration guaranteed the lasting enmity of Jews toward their Roman conquerors, even though Roman rule brought a much-needed measure of political stability. The hope for a deliverer, the Messiah promised in Scripture, became a major factor in Jewish thoughts and prayers.

How might the events of this period have helped prepare the world for the coming of Christ and the spread of the gospel?

_____

_____

40–50 MINUTES INTO THE WORD

"But when the time had fully come, God sent his Son, born of a woman, born under law, to redeem those under law, that we might receive the full rights of sons." Galatians 4:4, 5

Jesus was born, not just in a stable in Bethlehem, but into a world remarkably ready for his appearing.

- Centuries of unrest and periodic oppression fed the Jewish longing for the Messiah.
- Greek philosophy and learning had permeated the Middle East, contributing to a growing sense of dissatisfaction with the ancient religions.
- The Greek language had become the commonly used language of commerce and literature. The New Testament (and the Greek translation of the Old Testament) could be easily transcribed, disseminated, and understood by vast numbers of people.
- The Roman control of the Mediterranean world provided stability and an unparalleled transportation network by which people could travel more safely and efficiently than at any other period in the ancient world. Thus, the spread of the gospel took place via Roman roads and shipping lanes.

Truly, God had prepared the way for the remarkable entry of his son into human history and hearts.

10 MINUTES   **Step 1:   The Four Gospels**

Leader Notes

> Briefly introduce the four Gospels. Then have people work in pairs or trios to locate and read one of the references that describe the purpose or theme of that Gospel.

In explaining and defending their faith, the Gospel writers looked back to Old Testament prophecies of Jesus' life, death, and resurrection (i.e., Psalm 69:21, Isaiah 53; Micah 5:2). They recorded many of Jesus' sayings and deeds to explain their faith in him as God's Son. We read of Jesus' proclamation of the gospel ("good news") of the coming of God's kingdom. His ministry combined teaching and healing of both spiritual and physical ailments. His teaching followed that of the Old Testament prophets, and like them, he stirred up enemies. The Jewish religious leaders feared Jesus as a threat to their authority, and the Roman governor Pontius Pilate was persuaded to have Jesus executed. Thus, the Gospels present both the message of Jesus and the witness of others to his uniquely divine nature.

The first three Gospels (Matthew, Mark, and Luke) are very similar to each other and different from the Gospel of John. These three books are often called the Synoptic Gospels. While the word "synopsis," which is from the same roots (syn, "together"; optic, "view or sight"), refers to an outline or brief summary of a longer work, "synoptic" indicates agreement in point of view. Numerous events and teachings from the life of Jesus are recorded in two, and sometimes all three of the Synoptic Gospels. In spite of the many similarities, each of the Gospels has distinct qualities, which readers soon learn to notice and appreciate.

Matthew. **Matthew** was written for a Jewish-Christian audience to show that Jesus is the Messiah foretold in the Old Testament. More than any of the other Gospels, Matthew quotes Scripture to support Jesus' claim that he was the fulfillment of the prophecies. The writer is Matthew (Levi), a tax collector who was one of Jesus' disciples.

Mark. **Mark** is both the shortest of the four Gospels and the most focused on action. Although almost all of Mark is contained in the other Gospels, the quick pace of this story conveys a unique sense of urgency. Words and phrases such as "immediately" (eleven times), "as soon as" (seven times), and "at once" (seven times) appear more frequently in Mark than in the other Gospels. The author is John Mark. Some think he may possibly be the young man who fled the scene of Jesus' arrest (Mark 14:51, 52). Mark was a companion of Barnabas and Paul, and later of Peter. Many scholars see Peter as the actual source of most of the narratives recounted here.

Luke. **Luke** is the result of the writer's research. It recounts some stories not mentioned by any of the other three Gospels. Some of these events (e.g., Mary's visit to Elizabeth, the birth of John the Baptist, the shepherds and angels) are likely to have been told to the writer by Mary, the mother of Jesus. This book was obviously written by the same person who wrote **Acts**, and that person was Paul's loyal friend, Luke. Luke was probably a Gentile, a doctor, and very familiar with Greek culture.

John. The book of **John** is vastly different from the Synoptic Gospels. Most of the narrative takes place in Jerusalem. Few of Jesus' healing miracles are described. Neither are there many of the short parables that mark the teaching passages in the Synoptics. Instead, this Gospel is filled with extended discourses. It seems obvious that the writer, the apostle John, was very close to Jesus and sought to convey not just what Jesus said and did, but the significance of his words and actions.

❑ Locate each of the verses below and describe the purpose or theme of each Gospel.

Divide and Locate: Another Way to Find Bible References

To quickly locate references in the Gospels, divide the Bible in half (Psalms), then divide the second half in half again. In most Bibles, you will be in or near Matthew, the first New Testament book. From here, just turn toward the back to page through Mark, Luke, and then John.

KEY VERSES	PURPOSES OR THEMES
Matthew 1:22	
Mark 1:1,14, 15	
Luke 1:3, 4	
John 20:31	

10 MINUTES   **Step 2:   Jesus' Birth and Boyhood**

Leader Notes

Introduce the two accounts of Jesus' childhood. Then with people in the same pairs or trios, divide the class in half. Assign half of the groups to read one of the passages while the other half reads the other. Working together, have the pairs answer the questions below. Invite volunteers from each half of the room to share their answers.

The Gospels are not biographies of Jesus. They tell us nothing of what he looked like, how his voice sounded, or how tall he was. We see only fragments of his childhood, then nothing at all about most of the years he lived. As if cutting out everything that is extraneous to the purpose at hand, the writers show us only a select, limited number of incidents, those that illustrate the reason he came.

It is easy to see why the writers chose to tell about Jesus' teachings and miracles, his death, and his resurrection. It really is no surprise that Mark and John begin their accounts with Jesus as an adult, moving directly into the events of his ministry. But why did Matthew and Luke choose to include brief stories of his birth and childhood? What purpose is accomplished by reading of shepherds, or wise men, or a twelve-year-old's visit to the temple?

❏ Read Matthew 1:18-25 or Luke 2:1-7, then answer the following questions:

1. What reasons could there be for the Gospels to include these stories?

_____

_____

_____

2. What value do you find in knowing these facts about Jesus?

_____

_____

_____

Step 3: Jesus' Ministry and Teaching

Jesus' active ministry spanned just a little more than three years. During that time, he traveled relatively short distances, walking in and around Galilee, Samaria, and Judea. Still, his teachings covered a host of topics and concerns. The Gospels present Jesus' teaching, not in systematic fashion, but usually in response to the situations, people, and questions Jesus encountered. Thus, to explore Jesus' teachings, one of the most fruitful approaches is to select a topic, then study all that Jesus said about it. This can be done in several ways:

Concordance. A concordance is an alphabetical list of words in a book such as the Bible with brief excerpts and references of the words' occurrences. For example:

SCRIPTURE (SCRIPTURES)
Jn 2:22   Then they believed the *S*
   7:42   Does not the *S* say that the Christ

To use a concordance to explore a topic, just look up key words and see if there are any occurrences of its use.

NOTE: A concordance in the back of a Bible contains only selected words and excerpts.

Cross References. Many Bibles have cross references in the margin or at the bottom of the page. A cross reference leads you to other verses that deal with the same words or ideas. Different Bibles use their own cross-referencing systems. Commonly, special characters are placed by words or phrases in the text, and matching characters in the margin list related references.

Subject Index/Topical Bible. Some "study" Bibles include an alphabetical listing of important subjects with selected verse references under each subject. Topical Bibles are more extensive resources that group verses and passages under alphabetical topical headings.

Leader Notes

> Continuing with people in the same pairs or trios, have each small group choose any three of the references on Worksheet 4.1 to find one or more important truths about the Bible from the teachings of Jesus. Then have volunteers share any insights about Scripture they gained from their reading.

What Did Jesus Say About the Bible?

❏ Refer to **Worksheet 4.1 (p. 69)**. Read any three of the references listed under the heading, "What Did Jesus Say About the Bible?" Write down one or more important truths about the Bible.

10–15 MINUTES **Step 4:   Jesus' Death and Resurrection**

The dominant theme of the Gospels is that Jesus is the Christ (from the Greek word that translated the Hebrew title Messiah, meaning "the anointed one"). During Jesus' ministry, his followers had declared him to be the Christ, but they became fully convinced of this by his return to life after being killed on a Roman cross. Thus, the second major theme of the Gospels is the linking of suffering and resurrection. The Christ was not a violent conqueror, a mighty king wielding military and political power. Instead, Christ is a crucified Lord whose death and resurrection dramatically changed our world forever.

Leader Notes

Lead the class in another topical study. This time ask each individual to locate any two of the references on Worksheet 4.1 about Jesus' death and resurrection. If your class is large, have one-third of the people choose from the top of the list, one-third from the middle, and one-third from the bottom. After allowing time for people to locate and read their verses, invite volunteers to read aloud the verses they chose.

What Did Jesus Say About His Death and Resurrection?

❏ Read any two of the references on **Worksheet 4.1 (p. 69)** under the heading, "What Did Jesus Say About His Death and Resurrection?" Write down one or more important truths about Jesus' death and resurrection.

10–15 MINUTES **INTO LIFE**

Jesus spoke often about having been sent by the Father. His awareness of his unique mission was central to all he said and did. Every believer can gain a great deal of insight and guidance from a study of the things Jesus said about the purpose of his ministry.

Leader Notes Ask four volunteers to each read aloud one of the verses on Worksheet 4.1 in which Jesus stated his purpose in coming to our world. Next, ask the questions that follow, and invite responses from the group. Then, invite class members to write one action they believe they should take as a result of what they have seen in the Gospels. Finally, close in prayer.

What Did Jesus Say About His Purpose?

❑ Find and read the four passages listed on **Worksheet 4.1 (p. 70)** under the heading, "What Did Jesus Say About His Purpose?" Then answer the questions that follow.

❑ Take time to pray, asking to learn about yourself and about God from the example of Jesus.

WORKSHEET 4.1

What Did Jesus Say About the Bible?

Read any three of these references and write down one or more important truths about the Bible:

- Matthew 5:17-20
- Matthew 7:12
- Matthew 15:3-9
- Matthew 22:29
- Matthew 26:52-56
- Mark 12:29-31

- Luke 4:16-21
- Luke 24:25-27
- Luke 24:44-47
- John 5:39
- John 10:35
- John 16:24, 25

What insights about Scripture do you gain from Jesus' words?

_____

_____

What Did Jesus Say About His Death and Resurrection?

Read any two of these references and write down one or more important truths about Jesus' death and resurrection:

- Matthew 12:40
- Matthew 17:9
- Matthew 26:26-29, 32
- Mark 14:6-9
- Luke 9:22
- Luke 18:31-33
- Luke 24:44-48
- John 2:19

- John 3:14-16
- John 10:9-11
- John 10:14-18
- John 11:25, 26
- John 12:23, 24, 32
- John 14:28-31
- John 16:16, 22

What insights about Jesus' death and resurrection do you gain from what Jesus said?

_____

_____

What Did Jesus Say About His Purpose?

Find and read these four passages. Then answer the questions that follow.

- Mark 1:38
- Luke 5:31, 32
- John 3:17
- John 10:10b ("b" refers to the second half of a verse)

1. In light of these four statements, how would you explain why Jesus came?

_____

_____

_____

2. Having read Jesus' declarations of purpose, what do you believe he desires from those who follow him?

_____

_____

_____

Write one action you feel you should take this week as a result of what you have seen in the Gospels.

_____

_____

_____

LESSON 5

The Growth of the Church

When people first discover the fifth book of the New Testament, they tend to ask, in one form or another, the same question: "What kind of name for a book is 'Acts'?"

The question is not a complaint. Some are surprised to discover the real spelling of the book they've always thought was named after a hatchet. Others, after struggling with the long names of other books (e.g., Deuteronomy, Ecclesiastes, Zephaniah), are relieved to find a book with such a concise title: Acts. That's nice and simple. But what does it mean?

Many Bibles use longer titles for this book: "The Acts of the Apostles" or "The Acts of the Holy Spirit Through the Apostles." So, we know that the book of Acts is about the deeds the apostles accomplished in the power of the Holy Spirit. But who were the apostles?

The word "apostles" means people who are sent. The book of Acts features two apostles: Peter, outstanding leader of the fledgling church, and Paul, apostle to the Gentiles. It also tells some acts of other people, such as Stephen and Philip, Christians who cared for the needy and forcefully preached the good news. A study of their acts provides rich insight into the challenges of the Christian life and the power of the gospel.

LESSON 5—THE GROWTH OF THE CHURCH

OUTLINE

- The Ascension and Pentecost
- The Church in Jerusalem
- The Church Is Scattered
- Paul's Journeys

LEARNING ACTIVITIES

❏ Throughout this lesson you will find a variety of helpful learning activities indicated by a check box ❏. Mark the check box when you complete each activity.

LESSON TIME: 60–75 minutes

10–15 MINUTES ## INTO THE LESSON

Getting on the Map

> **Leader Notes**
>
> Provide a large map of the Mediterranean world in Bible times. Mount it on the front wall of the classroom. On 3" x 5" index cards, letter the locations and references listed below. As people arrive, distribute the cards among pairs or trios, instructing people to look up the Bible references and then locate the places on the map.
>
> OPTION: Provide lengths of colored yarn and pins or tape. Have people attach one end of a piece of yarn to the place they were assigned, then stretch the other end to the edge of the map where they attach it and the 3" x 5" card.

❏ Refer to **Worksheet 5.1 (p. 81)**. On the map of the Mediterranean area, locate at least three of the places listed on the worksheet. These places are mentioned prominently in the book of Acts. Look up the accompanying references to gain a sense of why these places are important to the story of the early believers.

❑ Locate and read Acts 1:8. What does Jesus' promise have to do with the places you located on Worksheet 5.1?

_____

_____

40–45 MINUTES INTO THE WORD

Acts was written as a sequel to the Gospel of Luke. Beginning in chapter 16, a number of incidents use the personal pronoun "we," indicating that the writer is now giving an eyewitness description of those incidents. All events prior to the account of Paul and his party's departure for Macedonia (16:10) were evidently learned from someone else. Whether the product of Luke's research or Luke's personal experience, Acts reveals insights into the formation of the earliest churches in Palestine and the eastern Mediterranean. In doing so, the book gives many vivid details of Paul's three great missionary journeys through which we are able to observe the dramatic spread of Christianity throughout the Roman empire.

The first half of Acts (1–12) deals with the establishment of the church and its initial efforts to share the good news of Jesus. The second half of the book (13–28) focuses on the ministry of Paul, the great apostle to the Gentiles. Immense tension is felt throughout these chapters as Paul seeks to maintain continuity with his Jewish heritage, yet at the same time defend his commitment that the basis for acceptance by God is faith in Jesus Christ.

10–15 MINUTES Step 1: The Ascension and Pentecost

Leader Notes

Briefly introduce the book of Acts and the benefits Bible readers and students can gain from comparing the same passage in two or more translations. Then have people form groups of no more than five per group and read the two passages from Peter's sermon, shown on Worksheet 5.2, comparing the wording of the different translations.

The first two chapters of Acts form a breathtaking link between the story of the Gospels and the story of the church. The reader who finishes the story of Jesus' life, death, and resurrection may feel as though a zenith has been reached. Anything that follows is bound to be anti-climactic, certainly less dramatic.

Such is not the case. As readers, we are quickly swept along with the action. The first amazing event is the ascension of Jesus into heaven.

❏ Read Acts 1:8-11. Imagine the scene that prompted the angel's question in verse 11. What thoughts do you suppose were going through the disciples' minds at that moment?

After the ascension, we are stunned by the exciting and miraculous sights and sounds of Pentecost:

- Wind and fire that marked the Holy Spirit's presence (2:1-3);
- The proclamation of the gospel in languages the speakers had never learned (2:4-12);
- The transformation of Peter from a man who denied he even knew Jesus into a bold proclaimer of the good news (2:14).

Comparing Translations

We live at a time when there are many Bible translations available, and many people own at least several. This can sometimes be confusing, yet it also has great advantages. To the vast majority of Bible readers who do not speak or read either Greek or Hebrew, comparing two or more translations of the same passage is often a very helpful way to study the Bible. Such comparison provides several benefits:

- It clarifies meaning and reduces misunderstanding. When a passage is not clear at first reading, reading it in another translation often helps illuminate the text.
- It reinforces the point. Having the same point made again, whether with different, similar, or even identical words, gives another chance to think about the passage's meaning and significance.
- It stimulates a fresh perspective. Especially with familiar passages, a different way of stating the

idea catches attention, keeping the reader from taking a passage for granted.

❏ In each of the three translations printed (and a fourth if you have one with you) read the excerpt on **Worksheet 5.2 (p. 82)** from Peter's message on the Day of Pentecost. Then answer the question that follows.

❏ Read each of the translations printed (and a fourth if you have one with you) on **Worksheet 5.3 (p. 83)** of the conclusion of Peter's message. This verse is often quoted as a central declaration of the response we must make to the news of Jesus' death and resurrection. Then answer the questions that follow.

10 MINUTES **Step 2: The Church in Jerusalem**

Leader Notes

Summarize the story of the early days of the church in Jerusalem. Then have the small groups compare the wording of different translations of Peter's response to the high priest's command that the apostles stop teaching about Jesus.

After Peter's sermon at Pentecost, 3,000 new believers were added to the number of those who followed Jesus (Acts 2:41). No organized plan was in place for nurturing the faith of these people. Immediately, however, the apostles began teaching all that they knew about Jesus. They included the new believers in regular fellowship, sharing of belongings, eating of meals (probably including observances of the Lord's Supper), and prayer. Regular meetings were held in the temple courts and in people's homes, and with every day that passed, even more people were being saved (Acts 2:42-47).

The dramatic healing of a crippled beggar at one of the temple gates (Acts 3:1-10) mobilized the opposition. The large crowd that gathered around Peter and John in the temple court was too much for the temple authorities to tolerate (Acts 3:11–4:3). This began a series of increasingly intense confrontations between the apostles and the religious authorities. Rather than extinguishing the fervor of Jesus' followers, however, even more conversions resulted (Acts 4:4; 5:13, 14).

4: 1-22
5: 17-
20
27-32
40-42

❑ Refer to **Worksheet 5.4 (p. 84)**. Read Peter's response to the high priest's complaint that the apostles had defied the order not to teach about Jesus. Many similar declarations in Acts summarize the apostles' beliefs. Then answer the questions that follow.

10–15 MINUTES **Step 3:   The Church Is Scattered**

Leader Notes

Explain how persecution that was intended to put an end to the church in Jerusalem actually resulted in the spread of the gospel to new areas. Next, have small groups compare translations of Peter's words in the house of the Roman official, Cornelius. (See Worksheet 5.5.) Then have the groups discuss the questions that follow.

Although Jesus had told his followers they would be his witnesses "to the ends of the earth" (Acts 1:8), the early believers developed no plan to share their faith with anyone other than people nearby. There were still plenty of opportunities in Jerusalem to reach people (Acts 6:7), and there seemed ample reason to continue to focus on local needs. Until, that is, the opposition to the growing church turned violent. Stephen, one of seven men chosen by the church to care for the needy, stirred up a hornet's nest with his powerful preaching. Finally, a mob stoned him to death (Acts 6, 7). In that mob was a young Pharisee named Saul (Acts 7:57–8:1). He did not actually pick up any stones, but he clearly approved of the attack.

That event launched a sharply escalating persecution of the church, led by Saul, which resulted in men and women being locked into prison. Far more significantly, the persecution scattered the believers, but not the apostles, throughout Judea and Samaria (Acts 8:1-5). When the apostles heard of the host of new believers being won outside the city, they went out to help with teaching in other places (Acts 8:14; 9:32).

Seeking to stamp out the spreading firestorm of evangelism, Saul also set out. He traveled to Damascus intending to bring back to Jerusalem any "who belonged to the Way" (Acts 9:1, 2). On the way, he had a life-changing encounter with Jesus (Acts 9:3-19). Within days, the greatest enemy of the church began to spread the news "that Jesus is the Son of God" (Acts 9:20).

As remarkable as Saul's conversion was, an equally dramatic change occurred in the attitudes toward Gentiles among Jewish followers of Jesus. Peter had a vision that rocked the very foundation of his view of God's love for all of humanity. After this vision, he entered a Roman soldier's house and shared the good news.

❏ Read Peter's words to Cornelius, the Roman officer on **Worksheet 5.5 (p. 86)**. Then answer the questions that follow.

10 MINUTES   ## Step 4: Paul's Journeys

Leader Notes

> Refer to the map of the Mediterranean area (Worksheet 5.1) and give a brief overview of Paul's four journeys. Next, have small groups compare versions of the conclusion of Paul's message to King Agrippa (Worksheet 5.6). Then have the groups discuss the questions that follow.
>
> NOTE: Retain the map for use again in Lesson 6.

Because of the rapid growth of the church in Antioch, the leaders in Jerusalem sent Barnabas to guide the new believers. Because he needed additional help, Barnabas located Saul and for a year the two men ministered together in that city (Acts 11:19-26).

Journey #1. (Acts 13-14) Toward the end of that year, the Holy Spirit guided the Antioch believers to send Barnabas and Saul to spread the good news in Cyprus (Acts 13:1-4). While in Cyprus, Saul began using his Roman name, Paul. From Cyprus, they sailed north to present-day Turkey, traveling inland to the province of Pisidia. They went first to the Jewish synagogue in each community, but after meeting repeated opposition, they finally announced, "we now turn to the Gentiles" (Acts 13:46). After visiting a series of towns, Barnabas and Paul retraced their journey so they could encourage those who had believed their message, both Jews and Gentiles.

Journey #2. (Acts 15-18) Paul and Barnabas reported to the church leaders in Jerusalem of the many Gentiles who had been converted. The council issued guidelines for these believers, clearly defining that keeping the Jewish law was not a requirement for life in Christ (Acts 15:19-21). After returning to Antioch, Paul and Barnabas had a sharp disagreement over their next journey, so they separated. Paul chose Silas to accompany him (Acts 15:36-41). Paul and Silas traveled to the towns Paul and Barnabas had visited in Pisidia, then pushed on through Galatia to the coast of the Aegean Sea (Acts 16:1-8). It was there that Paul had a vision of a Macedonian man asking for his help. Paul and several others crossed over into Macedonia, where they preached in Philippi, Thessalonica, and Berea, then moved south into Greece, preaching in the major cities of Athens and Corinth, before returning to Antioch (Acts 18:22).

Journey #3. (Acts 18:23–21:32) Once again Paul set off through the interior of Asia Minor. He traveled all the way to Ephesus, where he spent the next two years (Acts 19). He then journeyed back up through Macedonia, down into Greece, and then retraced the same roads. This time, instead of returning to Antioch, Paul went to Jerusalem, in spite of warnings that he would be in great danger. In Jerusalem, a crowd seized him inside the temple, dragged him outside, and attempted to kill him. Only the intervention of Roman soldiers stopped the beating (Acts 21:32).

Journey to Rome. (Acts 21:33–28:31) Paul's arrest by Roman soldiers set in motion a series of events that culminated in his being taken to Rome for a hearing, a privilege Paul claimed as a Roman citizen. First, while in custody, he had several opportunities to proclaim his faith to two Roman governors (Felix and Festus) and to Herod Agrippa II, great grandson of Herod the Great (Acts 24–26). Finally, the order was issued that Paul be taken to Rome. They traveled by sea. A severe storm almost killed all aboard the ship (Acts 27), but he finally arrived at Rome (Acts 28). Acts ends with Paul kept under guard in a rented home, but still able to boldly teach about Jesus.

❑ Read Paul's words to Agrippa on **Worksheet 5.6 (p. 89)**. Then answer the questions that follow.

10–15 MINUTES **INTO LIFE**

One of the most helpful exercises in thinking about the meaning and implication of a Scripture passage is to write or say it in your own words. Often it helps to think of a person to whom you would like to explain the passage, then write it so it would be clearly understood by that person.

Leader Notes

Divide the class into thirds. Assign the small groups in each section one of the verses on Worksheet 5.7. Ask the group members to work together and write the verse in their own words. After several minutes, invite volunteers to read aloud what their groups have written.

❏ Read one of the verses on **Worksheet 5.7 (p. 91)**, then write it in your own words as you might state it for someone who had never heard about how to become a Christian.

As You Near the Completion of This Brief Study

❏ Refer to the booklet, *The Bible: Easy Access Guide*. Review it as a helpful summary of key points covered in this course.

❏ Continue a regular Bible study plan such as "A One-Month Introduction to Your Bible" in the *Easy Access Guide* booklet.

❏ Conclude this study with prayer, asking God to help you continue to explore and apply the truths of God's Word.

Why Study Acts?

WORKSHEET 5.1

On the map of the Mediterranean area below, locate at least three of the following places mentioned prominently in the book of Acts. Look up the accompanying references to gain a sense of why these places are important to the story of the early believers.

- Jerusalem (Acts 1:4)
- Samaria (Acts 8:5)
- Damascus (Acts 9:2)
- Caesarea (Acts 10:1)
- Antioch (Acts 11:19, 20)
- Cyprus (Acts 13:4, 5)
- Pisidian Antioch (Acts 13:14, 15)

- Philippi (Acts 16:12)
- Thessalonica (Acts 17:1)
- Athens (Acts 17:16)
- Corinth (Acts 18:1)
- Ephesus (Acts 19:1, 2)
- Rome (Acts 28:16)

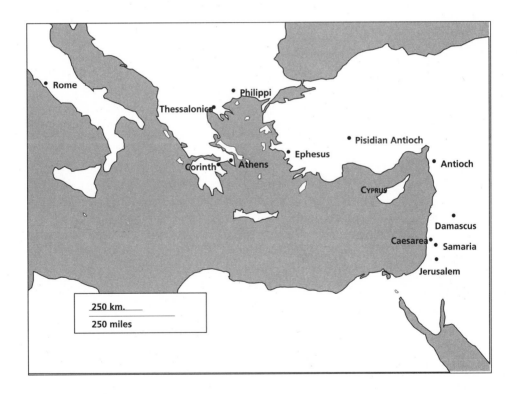

WORKSHEET 5.2

In each of the three translations printed (and a fourth if you have one with you) read the following excerpt from Peter's message on the Day of Pentecost. Then answer the question that follows.

ACTS 2:22–24		
KING JAMES VERSION	**NEW INTERNATIONAL VERSION**	**THE MESSAGE**
"Ye men of Israel, hear these words;	"Men of Israel, listen to this:	"Fellow Israelites, listen carefully to these words:
Jesus of Nazareth, a man approved of God among you by miracles and wonders and signs, which God did by him in the midst of you, as ye yourselves also know:	Jesus of Nazareth was a man accredited by God to you by miracles, wonders and signs, which God did among you through him, as you yourselves know.	Jesus the Nazarene, a man thoroughly accredited by God to you—the miracles and wonders and signs that God did through him are common knowledge—
him, being delivered by the determinate counsel and foreknowledge of God,	This man was handed over to you by God's set purpose and foreknowledge;	this Jesus, following the deliberate and well-thought-out plan of God,
ye have taken, and by wicked hands have crucified and slain:	and you, with the help of wicked men, put him to death by nailing him to the cross.	was betrayed by men who took the law into their own hands, and was handed over to you. And you pinned him to a cross and killed him.
whom God hath raised up, having loosed the pains of death: because it was not possible that he should be holden of it."	But God raised him from the dead, freeing him from the agony of death, because it was impossible for death to keep its hold on him."	But God untied the death ropes and raised him up. Death was no match for him."

What idea stands out to you more strongly after the third reading than after the first?

_____

_____

_____

WORKSHEET 5.3

Read each of the translations printed (and a fourth if you have one with you) of the conclusion of Peter's message. This verse is often quoted as a central declaration of the response we must make to the news of Jesus' death and resurrection. Then answer the questions that follow.

ACTS 2:38		
KING JAMES VERSION	**NEW INTERNATIONAL VERSION**	**THE MESSAGE**
"Then Peter said unto them,	"Peter replied,	"Peter said,
Repent, and be baptized every one of you	'Repent and be baptized, every one of you,	'Change your life. Turn to God and be baptized, each of you,
in the name of Jesus Christ for the remission of sins,	in the name of Jesus Christ for the forgiveness of your sins.	in the name of Jesus Christ, so your sins are forgiven.
and ye shall receive the gift of the Holy Ghost."	And you will receive the gift of the Holy Spirit.'"	Receive the gift of the Holy Spirit.'"

1. How does the paraphrase "Change your life. Turn to God" affect your understanding of the word "repent"?

_____

_____

_____

2. Which word is more meaningful to you: "remission" or "forgiveness"? Why?

_____

_____

_____

WORKSHEET 5.4

Read Peter's response to the high priest's complaint that the apostles had defied the order not to teach about Jesus. Many similar declarations in Acts summarize the apostles' beliefs. Then answer the questions that follow.

ACTS 5:29-32		
KING JAMES VERSION	**NEW INTERNATIONAL VERSION**	**THE MESSAGE**
"Then Peter and the other apostles answered and said,	"Peter and the other apostles replied:	"Peter and the apostles answered,
We ought to obey God rather than men.	'We must obey God rather than men!	'It's necessary to obey God rather than men.
The God of our fathers raised up Jesus, whom ye slew and hanged on a tree.	The God of our fathers raised Jesus from the dead—whom you had killed by hanging him on a tree.	The God of our ancestors raised up Jesus, the One you killed by hanging him on a cross.
Him hath God exalted with his right hand to be a Prince and a Saviour, for to give repentance to Israel, and forgiveness of sins.	God exalted him to his own right hand as Prince and Savior that he might give repentance and forgiveness of sins to Israel.	God set him on high at his side, Prince and Savior, to give Israel the gift of a changed life and sins forgiven.
And we are his witnesses of these things; and so is also the Holy Ghost, whom God hath given to them that obey him."	We are witnesses of these things, and so is the Holy Spirit, whom God has given to those who obey him.'"	And we are witnesses to these things. The Holy Spirit, whom God gives to those who obey him, corroborates every detail.'"

1. If you were a news reporter covering the apostles' appearance before the Sanhedrin (the high court of the Jews, with broad civil and religious authority under Roman rule), how would you explain Peter's beliefs?

_____

_____

_____

2. What significance does Peter's declaration have for you and your faith?

_____

_____

_____

WORKSHEET 5.5

Read Peter's words to Cornelius, the Roman officer. Then answer the questions that follow.

ACTS 10:34–43		
KING JAMES VERSION	**NEW INTERNATIONAL VERSION**	**THE MESSAGE**
"Then Peter opened his mouth, and said, Of a truth I perceive that God is no respecter of persons:	"Then Peter began to speak: 'I now realize how true it is that God does not show favoritism	"Peter fairly exploded with his good news: 'It's God's own truth, nothing could be plainer: God plays no favorites!
but in every nation he that feareth him, and worketh righteousness, is accepted with him.	but accepts men from every nation who fear him and do what is right.	It makes no difference who you are or where you're from—if you want God and are ready to do as he says, the door is open.
The word which God sent unto the children of Israel, preaching peace by Jesus Christ: (he is Lord of all:)	You know the message God sent to the people of Israel, telling the good news of peace through Jesus Christ, who is Lord of all.	The Message he sent to the children of Israel—that through Jesus Christ every thing is being put together again—well, he's doing it everywhere, among everyone.
that word, I say, ye know, which was published throughout all Judea, and began from Galilee, after the baptism which John preached;	You know what has happened throughout Judea, beginning in Galilee after the baptism that John preached—	You know the story of what happened in Judea. It began in Galilee after John preached a total life-change.
How God anointed Jesus of Nazareth with the Holy Ghost and with power: who went about doing good, and healing all that were oppressed of the devil; for God was with him.	how God anointed Jesus of Nazareth with the Holy Spirit and power, and how he went around doing good and healing all who were under the power of the devil, because God was with him.	Then Jesus arrived from Nazareth, anointed by God with the Holy Spirit, ready for action. He went through the country helping people and healing everyone who was beaten down by the Devil. He was able to do all this because God was with him.

continued

ACTS 10:34-43		
KING JAMES VERSION	**NEW INTERNATIONAL VERSION**	**THE MESSAGE**
And we are witnesses of all things which he did both in the land of the Jews, and in Jerusalem; whom they slew and hanged on a tree:	We are witnesses of everything he did in the country of the Jews and in Jerusalem. They killed him by hanging him on a tree,	And we saw it, saw it all, everything he did in the land of the Jews and in Jerusalem where they killed him, hung him from a cross.
him God raised up the third day, and showed him openly;	but God raised him from the dead on the third day and caused him to be seen.	But in three days God had him up, alive, and out where he could be seen.
not to all the people, but unto witnesses chosen before of God, even to us, who did eat and drink with him after he rose from the dead.	He was not seen by all the people, but by witnesses whom God had already chosen—by us who ate and drank with him after he rose from the dead.	Not everyone saw him—he wasn't put on public display. Witnesses had been carefully handpicked by God beforehand—us! We were the ones, there to eat and drink with him after he came back from the dead.
And he commanded us to preach unto the people, and to testify that it is he which was ordained of God to be the Judge of quick and dead.	He commanded us to preach to the people and to testify that he is the one whom God appointed as judge of the living and the dead.	He commissioned us to announce this in public, to bear solemn witness that he is in fact the One whom God destined as Judge of the living and dead.
To him give all the prophets witness, that through his name whosoever believeth in him shall receive remission of sins."	All the prophets testify about him that everyone who believes in him receives forgiveness of sins through his name.'"	But we're not alone in this. Our witness that he is the means to forgiveness of sins is backed up by the witness of all the prophets.'"

continued

1. How convincing is Peter in declaring that God views all people equally? (Remember that just a few hours before this, Peter would have refused to have any dealings with any non-Jew, especially a Roman.)

_____

_____

_____

2. What points does Peter repeat from his earlier declarations about Jesus?

_____

_____

_____

3. What does Peter add here to his earlier statements about the central issues of the faith?

_____

_____

_____

4. Which sentence or phrase in the above statement stands out as something important for you to remember?

_____

_____

_____

WORKSHEET 5.6

Read Paul's words to Agrippa. Then answer the questions that follow.

ACTS 26:22, 23		
KING JAMES VERSION	**NEW INTERNATIONAL VERSION**	**THE MESSAGE**
"Having therefore obtained help of God,	"But I have had God's help to this very day,	But God has stood by me, just as he promised,
I continue unto this day, witnessing both to small and great,	and so I stand here and testify to small and great alike.	and I'm standing here saying what I've been saying to anyone, whether king or child, who will listen.
saying none other things than those which the prophets and Moses did say should come:	I am saying nothing beyond what the prophets and Moses said would happen—	And everything I'm saying is completely in line with what the prophets and Moses said would happen:
that Christ should suffer, and that he should be the first that should rise from the dead,	that the Christ would suffer and, as the first to rise from the dead,	One, the Messiah must die; two, raised from the dead,
and should show light unto the people, and to the Gentiles."	would proclaim light to his own people and to the Gentiles."	he would be the first rays of God's daylight shining on people far and near, people both godless and God-fearing."

1. After hearing Paul say this, why do you suppose Governor Festus accused Paul of being out of his mind, but Agrippa asked, "Do you think that in such a short time you can persuade me to be a Christian?"

_____

_____

_____

2. Why do you think Paul, Peter, and the other apostles kept repeating this same basic message over and over?

_____

_____

_____

3. What truth about Jesus stands out to you as being the most important thing the early Christians believed about him?

_____

_____

_____

WORKSHEET 5.7

Read one of these verses, then write it in your own words as you might state it for someone who had never heard about how to become a Christian.

ACTS 3:19		
KING JAMES VERSION	**NEW INTERNATIONAL VERSION**	**WRITE IT IN YOUR OWN WORDS**
"Repent ye therefore, and be converted, that your sins may be blotted out."	"Repent, then, and turn to God, so that your sins may be wiped out."	

ACTS 4:12		
KING JAMES VERSION	**NEW INTERNATIONAL VERSION**	**WRITE IT IN YOUR OWN WORDS**
"Neither is there salvation in any other: for there is none other name under heaven given among men, whereby we must be saved."	"'Salvation is found in no one else, for there is no other name under heaven given to men by which we must be saved.'"	

ACTS 16:31		
KING JAMES VERSION	**NEW INTERNATIONAL VERSION**	**WRITE IT IN YOUR OWN WORDS**
"Believe on the Lord Jesus Christ, and thou shalt be saved, and thy house."	"'Believe in the Lord Jesus, and you will be saved— you and your household.'"	

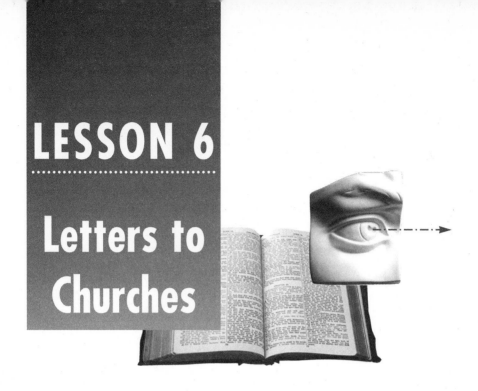

LESSON 6

Letters to Churches

"I feel like I know you, but I really don't know you very well," the young man said. Have you ever had a similar experience? Have you ever spent time with someone—a neighbor, coworker, relative, or family member—without really knowing what makes him or her tick?

The New Testament letters give us remarkable insights into the lives of the people to whom the letters were written. They also reveal a great deal about those who wrote them. Rather than telling us stories of what people did, these letters open up the hearts and minds of some fascinating people. The very personal nature of these letters makes their writers and readers become as real to us as those whose narratives are recorded elsewhere in Scripture.

But peeking inside the private thoughts and experiences of people who lived nearly two thousand years ago is not the major benefit of reading these letters. Even when the ink was barely dry on the original documents, these letters captivated interest because of what they reveal about God and his work in people's lives.

In the process of reading these letters, we also discover ourselves. The same issues, problems, and questions that confronted the early Christians are concerns of our lives as well. This lesson provides an overview of these remarkable documents, with an opportunity to explore two favorite passages in depth.

LESSON 6—LETTERS TO CHURCHES

OUTLINE

- Paul's Letters to Churches
- Paul's Pastoral Letters
- General Letters
- Revelation

LEARNING ACTIVITIES

❑ Throughout this lesson you will find a variety of helpful learning activities indicated by a check box ❑. Mark the check box when you complete each activity.

LESSON TIME: 60–75 minutes

10–15 MINUTES **INTO THE LESSON**

Scrambled Verses

The New Testament letters (epistles) are filled with notable statements that are quoted often and are well worth committing to memory. A wide range of theological and practical topics are addressed in these documents, sometimes in extended passages, but often with short, direct phrasing that sticks in the reader's mind. The following references all make strong declarations about Scripture, helping us see the high regard with which God's Word was held in the early church, and nudging us to make it a priority in our lives today.

Leader Notes

Before people arrive, letter each of the following references on the chalkboard or a poster. As people arrive, have them form groups of no more than four people per group. Give each group a sheet of colored poster board, a felt marking pen, and a pair of scissors. Assign each group one of the following references to learn. Have the groups look up their verse, copy it onto their poster, then cut their poster into twelve pieces. As soon as all groups have cut their poster apart and mixed up the pieces, have groups exchange pieces and then work to put them back into correct order. Have each group quote the verse they unscrambled.

❑ Look up and read one of these verses about Scripture. To help you memorize this verse, copy it onto a sheet of blank paper. Then cut the sheet into twelve pieces and mix up the pieces. Then put the verse back in the correct order. Finally, without looking at the verse, quote it aloud.

- Romans 15:4
- 1 Thessalonians 5:27
- 1 Timothy 4:13
- 2 Timothy 2:15
- 2 Timothy 3:16
- 2 Peter 1:19

40–45 MINUTES INTO THE WORD

Letters

Two kinds of letters are attributed to Paul: Letters to Churches and Pastoral Epistles. Starting with Romans, the first nine New Testament letters are generally attributed to Paul, and were addressed by him to people in specific churches. Paul was familiar with most of the places to which the letters were sent, having traveled to the areas on one or more of his extensive journeys. These letters deal mainly with issues of faith, morals, and daily living. Each letter emphasizes important issues of the Christian faith and specific instructions for dealing with a wide variety of practical problems.

Four letters are called Pastoral Epistles: 1 and 2 Timothy, Titus, and Philemon. These are addressed to individuals, but were also circulated among churches.

The general letters were written by several different authors, and were directed to the church as a whole, rather than to believers in a specific location.

Revelation

The book of Revelation was not really a letter, but it was circulated among the churches as were the epistles.

Step 1:   Paul's Letters to Churches

The Acrostic Plan for Locating Letters.   The Divide and Locate approach to locating Bible references still has value in exploring the New Testament letters. (They're in the final eighth of the Bible, not counting pages used for reference material such as a concordance, topical index, or maps.) However, if you find yourself opening the Bible to one of the letters, how do you know whether to go forward or backward to find the letter you want? Try using this acrostic to help you find your way among Paul's nine letters to churches: **RCCGEPCTT—R**eading **C**hristian **C**orrespondence **G**ives **E**veryone **P**lenty of **C**omfort, **T**ruth, and **T**raining. Obviously, these are the initials of the nine letters: Romans, 1 and 2 Corinthians, etc.

Inductive Study.   One of the most productive approaches to Bible study is called "inductive study." Using this method, the reader focuses on a specific passage, seeking to understand its content and meaning, then drawing conclusions only from what is stated there. Inductive study follows the basic format of four questions:

- What does the passage say?
- What does it mean?
- What does it mean to me?
- What should I do about it?

This method differs from looking at a passage to find support for conclusions already arrived at from other sources. In this session, the questions asked are intended to help you study several passages inductively.

Leader Notes

> Briefly introduce the nine letters of Paul to the churches, referring to the same map used in Lesson 5. Have people return to the small groups in which they began the session. Assign each group a selected reference from Worksheet 6.1 and have them read it and answer the questions that follow. After several minutes, invite volunteers to share their answers.

Romans was written before Paul had been to Rome, but he had heard a great deal about the believers in Rome (chapter 16). Romans provides the most extensive declaration in Scripture that everyone is a sinner and needs

salvation. **First and 2 Corinthians** are two of three letters Paul wrote to instruct the believers in Corinth. (The
third letter was an earlier note, which has not survived.
Paul mentions it in 1 Corinthians 5:9, 10.) Many problems existed within this congregation, including divisive-
ness, immorality, false teachers, and excesses in responding to the Holy Spirit's gifts. **Galatians** is often considered a "condensed" version of Romans, as it deals with
many of the same themes, but more briefly. **Ephesians**
was written while Paul was in prison and reflects the
deep affection Paul had for the people with whom he
had spent three years of ministry (Acts 20:31). The letter
explains the many benefits of salvation and provides
very practical instructions for all who seek to live as
Christ's people. **Philippians** was also written while Paul
was a prisoner. It expresses his very deep gratitude for
the encouragement and help the believers in Philippi
had given him. This letter is considered by many to be
the most uplifting of all the ones Paul wrote. **Colossians**
is very similar to Ephesians. Both letters were evidently
written at the same time and delivered by the same mes-
sengers. (The letter to **Philemon** was also carried at the
same time, as Philemon was a resident of Colosse.) **First
and 2 Thessalonians** focus on questions about the
return of Christ.

❑ **Worksheet 6.1 (p. 103)** lists a random sampling of
beloved quotations from Paul's letters to the churches.
Locate and read one verse, then answer the questions
that follow.

10 MINUTES   ### Step 2: Paul's Pastoral Letters

> Introduce each of these four brief letters. Read aloud Paul's letter to
> Philemon, then lead the class in responding to the questions that
> follow.

Timothy and **Titus** were young associates of Paul, each
of whom had pastoral responsibilities for a congregation.
These brief letters contain directions for church leaders
and warn against errors in doctrine and behavior.
Philemon was a believer in the church at Colosse. This

letter is an appeal by Paul on behalf of Philemon's former slave, Onesimus (meaning "useful"), who had run away from Philemon, then become a Christian through Paul's ministry while Paul was a prisoner in Rome.

❑ Read Paul's letter to Philemon, then respond to the questions below.

1. What does Paul say to affirm Philemon?

_____

_____

_____

2. What does Paul say about the runaway slave, Onesimus?

_____

_____

_____

3. On what does Paul base the request he makes of Philemon?

_____

_____

_____

4. What "benefit" (verse 20) is Paul asking for from Philemon?

_____

_____

_____

5. Compare your own life experience with that of Onesimus. In what ways might you have been described as "useless" before you found Christ? How have you become "useful" in your Christian life?

_____

_____

_____

15 MINUTES   **Step 3:   General Letters**

Leader Notes

> Introduce each of these eight letters. Then have small groups complete a brief inductive study of 1 John 1.

Hebrews is much more a sermon than a letter. Written by an unnamed author, it presents Christ as the perfect high priest, and urges faithfulness in a time of persecution. **James** contrasts good deeds against a claim to have faith that is not coupled with right action. **First and 2 Peter** proclaim joy in the face of persecution and warn against false teachers. The three letters by **John** emphasize the relationship between love for others and love for God. **Jude** also warns against false teachers.

❏ Read 1 John 1, then answer the following questions.

1.   What does John say he is proclaiming?

_____

_____

_____

2. What authority does John claim to be able to proclaim this?

_____

_____

_____

3. What are the purposes of John's proclamation?

_____

_____

_____

4. What actions does John compare with darkness and light?

_____

_____

_____

5. What contrasting results does John describe if we deny our sins or confess our sins?

_____

_____

_____

6. Based on this chapter what actions should we take?

_____

_____

_____

5 MINUTES   **Step 4:   Revelation**

Leader Notes

> Introduce this final book. Read aloud Revelation 1:1-8, and then ask volunteers to identify the descriptions of Christ contained in these verses.

The book of **Revelation** is addressed to churches in seven cities in the province of Asia (modern Turkey). It was written to encourage Christians to be faithful, probably during persecution under the emperor Domitian (A.D. 81–96). The future is described by the use of many symbols, describing God's judgment on evil, a thousand-year reign of Christ, and a new heaven and a new earth.

❏   Read Revelation 1:1-8, then list the various ways Christ is described in these verses:

_____

_____

_____

10–15 MINUTES   INTO LIFE

Leader Notes

> Review the guidelines for getting the most from studying the Bible that are listed in the *Easy Access Guide*. Encourage group members to select a Bible reading plan for at least the next month. Then have small groups pray for one another.

Gain Benefit From What You Read

There are many ways to gain the most benefit from your Bible reading.

- Pray before and after you read. The Bible is God's Word, so ask him to help you understand and apply it.
- Read any passages both before and after a group study. You get more out of the group meeting if you read the passages first, and you

get more out of the passages if you read them again afterward.

- When you read stories from the Bible, look for what you can learn from both positive and negative examples.

- When reading the words of Jesus or New Testament letters, imagine the words being spoken to you. Mentally insert your own name in some of the verses.

- Pause during and after reading to answer these three questions about what you have read: What does it mean? What does it mean to me? What do I need to do about it?

❏ Choose a Bible reading plan to follow for at least the next month. Consider these options:

- "A One-Month Introduction to Your Bible (30 Passages Everyone Should Read)." (See *The Bible: Easy Access Guide.*)

- Read one of the four Gospels (Matthew, Mark, Luke, or John). Divide the book into fourths, then read one-fourth at least two times each week. (Because Mark is brief and easy reading, it is a good choice as the first Gospel to read.)

- Read one of the New Testament letters. If you choose one of the longer letters (Romans, 1 or 2 Corinthians, Hebrews), plan to read it once each week for the month. If you choose one of the shorter letters, read it twice each week for the month. Or choose two of the shorter letters and alternate between the letters each week.

- Read Psalms and Proverbs. Each day read one of the following 31 Psalms (selected from the first 100) and a chapter from Proverbs.

  Psalm 1, 8, 15, 16, 18, 19, 20, 22, 23, 24, 25, 27, 30, 32, 33, 34, 37, 38, 40, 42, 46, 51, 65, 67, 72, 84, 90, 91, 95, 96, 100

❏ Take time to pray. Commit to the Lord your intention to continue reading his Word.

WORKSHEET 6.1

Below is a random sampling of beloved quotations from Paul's letters to the churches. Locate and read one verse, then answer the questions that follow.

- Romans 3:23, 24
- 1 Corinthians 13:1
- 2 Corinthians 3:18
- Galatians 2:20
- Ephesians 2:8, 9

- Philippians 4:8
- Colossians 2:6
- 1 Thessalonians 5:6-18
- 2 Thessalonians 2:16, 17

1. What is Paul saying here?

_____

_____

2. What is his main point?

_____

_____

3. If Paul had written this letter to the people in your church, how might he have worded it?

_____

_____

4. Imagine Paul saying this directly to you, then looking you in the eye and waiting for you to respond. What would you say to him?

_____

_____

How Did We Get Our Bible?

Is our Bible complete?
Is it accurate?
Can I depend on it?

> "I have hidden your word in my heart
> that I might not sin against you."
> Psalm 119:11

> "Your word is a lamp to my feet
> and a light for my path."
> Psalm 119:105

> "All Scripture is God-breathed and is useful for teaching,
> rebuking, correcting and training in righteousness."
> 2 Timothy 3:16

The Bible certainly makes lofty claims for itself: protection against sin, a reliable guide for living, God's own means to teach us his ways. This is not an ordinary book.

But how did sixty-six books written by more than forty authors separated by fifteen hundred years, come together into one book? And how do we know the book we read today is even remotely similar to the sacred writings of the ancient Hebrews and early Christians? How much confidence can we place in the English words we read? How do we know the passing of centuries and the vast cultural differences that separate us from the writers have not produced significant changes in the message of the book?

THE CANON

The ancient Jews and the early Christians produced many more writings than those collected in the Bible. Those that were recognized as truly being God's Word, and therefore acknowledged to belong among the sacred writings, are referred to as the "canon." This term is from the Latin and Greek words for rule, a device for measuring. Thus, the "canon" of Scripture refers to a specific standard that was set forth, and the "canonical" books were recognized as having met that standard. The standard is simple, yet profound: a writing had to be recognized as communicating God's revelation to humanity.

THE HEBREW BIBLE

The details of the process by which the Jewish canon was formed are lost in the mists of ancient history. It is certain that at least by the third century B.C., the present collection we know as the Old Testament was complete. At that time, a very influential Greek translation of the Hebrew Scriptures (the Septuagint, meaning "seventy") was produced by about seventy Jewish rabbis of Alexandria. This translation was widely used during the time of Christ and the early church, and made a clear distinction between the Septuagint and others, such as the Apocrypha (see the following page).

Several centuries before the rabbis did their work, after the years of exile, Ezra the scribe instituted major reforms, all based precisely in the books of the Law. Ezra is generally credited not only with effectively teaching the Scriptures and encouraging the people to obey them, but also with bringing together the present collection of writings. Whether this was the first time all or most of the books were assembled together, or whether Ezra simply regathered them after the decades of disaster, it is evident that Ezra and the people already had high regard for these writings.

Numerous other glimpses are given in the Old Testament that these books had long been esteemed by the Jewish people as being God's Word to them. There are no valid reasons to doubt Moses' significant involvement in writing down the words of the Law. Even as early as the time of Joshua we find numerous references attesting to the honor and respect people had for the books of the Law. While there were numerous times when Israel did not obey Scripture, there is no indication that the nation ever questioned its truth and authority.

What does all this mean? Simply that the books of the canon did not receive honor because they had made their way into a sacred collection. Rather, they were in the canon because they were perceived to be deserving of honor. The recognition that these were very special books preceded their being assembled together. In addition, Jesus and the early Christians accepted the Hebrew canon without question as "the very words of God" (Romans 3:2).

THE APOCRYPHA

Other ancient writings were valued, but not viewed as showing God's direct hand in their writing or their message. The books of the Apocrypha are included in Roman Catholic and Orthodox Bibles as deuterocanonical (added to the earlier canon), but have always been excluded from the Hebrew Bible and from most Protestant Bibles. (The term apocrypha means "hidden" or "secret.") The Apocrypha does provide important information about Jewish history and religious developments in the centuries before the birth of Christ. The books were gradually added to later editions of the Septuagint, but were always considered less authoritative than the biblical books. Even Jerome, who included them in his Latin translation of the Bible (the Vulgate) in the fifth century, pointed out various ways in which these books were of lesser quality than the canonical books. The Council of Trent in the sixteenth century, seeking to counter the growing influence of the Protestant reformers, proclaimed the Apocrypha to be fully sacred and canonical.

OTHER WRITINGS

Many other Jewish and Christian books were written between 200 B.C. and A.D. 200. Some of these contain fanciful legends, and some claimed to have been written by the apostles, but were obvious forgeries. Even so, they do throw light on Judaism, some of Jesus' teachings, and the early years of Christianity. Of far greater value, some leaders of the early church left pastoral writings that are similar in style and content to the New Testament. Some of the apostolic fathers, successors to the original apostles in leading the church, wrote helpful commentaries on New Testament books. For a period of time in some churches, certain of these works were studied enthusiastically, and even treated as Scripture.

THE CHRISTIAN BIBLE

While the Old Testament books were written over more than a thousand years, all the New Testament books were written within a few decades of each other. By early in the second century, twenty New Testament books were being widely circulated and honored as being of apostolic origin. Questions were raised about Hebrews because the author was unknown. The letters of James, 2 Peter, 2 and 3 John, and Jude were questioned by some because they were so short, because they were written later than the other epistles, or because James and Jude were not among the original apostles. Revelation was initially unanimously accepted, but doubts arose a century or two later. Finally, by the start of the fourth century, all debates had been resolved and the canon was complete.

THE YEARS IN BETWEEN

Until the invention of the printing press, every copy of the Bible had to be painstakingly lettered by hand. Both Hebrew and Christian scribes worked meticulously to preserve the exact rendering of the text from one copy to the next. During the past century numerous discoveries of ancient manuscripts have served to confirm the faith of Bible readers, showing only minimal, and usually inconsequential, differences in manuscripts separated by hundreds of years. Both Old and New Testaments have been preserved intact, enabling the modern day reader to receive the same message as the ancient Hebrew or the first-century Christian.

Glossary

Apocrypha   "Hidden" or "secret" — Fourteen Jewish books written between the Old and New Testament periods that were not part of the Hebrew Scriptures. Eleven of these are included in Roman Catholic Bibles.

Apostle   "Messenger" — Refers to the original twelve disciples and also others commissioned by the early church to spread the gospel.

Apostolic Fathers   Successors to the original apostles in leading the church.

Aramaic   The language of the common people in Palestine during the time of Christ; thus, it was the language he spoke.

Ascension   Jesus' return to Heaven forty days after his resurrection (Acts 1).

Baal   "Master" — Refers to false gods worshiped by the people of Canaan.

Babylon   Name of both a powerful empire and its capital city; conqueror of Judah.

Book   Any of the sixty-six separate writings that together make up the Bible.

Canaan   Early name for the territory between the Mediterranean Sea and the Jordan River.

Canon   "Standard," "rule," or "measure" — The sacred, biblical books recognized as those that communicate God's revelation to humanity.

Captivity   See *Exile*.

Chapter   A section within most books of the Bible. Chapters are further divided into verses. The chapter and verse divisions were made long after the Bible was written to help readers locate passages quickly.

Christ   "Anointed One" — The Greek term for the Hebrew title "Messiah"; the title given to the Savior God promised to send to earth.

Christians   "Belonging to Christ" — The name was first given to Jesus' followers in Antioch.

Concordance   An alphabetical index of the key words in the Bible that shows the occurrences and context of the words.

Covenant   "Agreement" — Usually refers to the promises God made with people and the responses he required of them.

Cross Reference   A note inserted in the margins or footnotes of a Bible that refers the reader to other passages dealing with the same topic.

Crucifixion   A painful form of execution used by the Romans in which a person was attached to a cross and left hanging on it until dead.

Deacon   "Servant" — A title given people who have been selected to provide help and leadership in the church. Stephen and Philip were two of the first deacons (Acts 6).

Defile   The act of making something unclean or unfit for sacred purposes.

Deuterocanonical   "Second canon" — The Apocrypha; books of the Old Testament that were added to, but not included with, the canon of the Hebrew Bible.

Disciple   "Learner" — A follower of Jesus, often used to refer to any of the twelve men he chose to accompany him during his years of ministry.

Epistle   "Letter" — Most of the New Testament books were written as letters to encourage and instruct churches and individuals.

Exile   A common practice in ancient warfare was for the victors to forcibly relocate defeated people into other lands. This was done to diminish the possibility of rebellion. Large numbers of people in both the northern kingdom of Israel and the southern kingdom of Judah were marched into captivity when defeated by Assyria and Babylon.

General Letters   The last eight New Testament books (excluding Revelation) were intended for distribution among churches in different areas. They were not written to any specific church or person.

Gentile   Any person who is not Jewish.

Gospel   "Good news" — The message that Jesus is God's Son who died and returned to life to bring forgiveness of sins.

Greek   The common language of the first-century Mediterranean world. It was widely used in commerce and was the language in which the New Testament was written.

Hebrew   The language in which the Old Testament was written.

Hebrews   Jewish people; a letter in the New Testament.

Holy Spirit   The powerful person of God at work in human lives; the third member, along with God the Father and Jesus the Son, of the Trinity.

Idolatry   The worship of idols (images).

Inductive Study   An approach to Bible study that seeks to gain understanding directly from the text at hand, rather than from sources outside the text itself.

Israel   "Prince with God" — The name God gave Jacob. It later became the name for the Hebrew nation. When the nation split into two kingdoms, the name referred to the northern kingdom.

Israelites   The people of Israel.

Jews   Originally referred to the tribe of Judah. After the exile, the name distinguished Hebrews from Gentiles.

Judah   One of Jacob's sons; thus, Judah was one of the twelve tribes of Israel. When the nation split into two kingdoms, the name was attached to the southern kingdom.

Judge   During the years after the Israelites settled Canaan, God selected and equipped leaders (judges) to rule the people, settle disagreements, and lead in worship. Repeatedly the judges had to call the people away from idolatry.

King James Version   A seventeenth-century English translation (also called *The Authorized Version*) of the Bible commissioned by King James I. For nearly four centuries it has been widely read and much beloved.

Levites   Descendants of Levi, who was one of Jacob's sons. All priests had to be Levites.

Major Prophets   The Old Testament books of Isaiah, Jeremiah, Lamentations, Ezekiel, and Daniel. These books are larger than those of the twelve Minor Prophets.

Messiah   See *Christ*.

Minor Prophets   See *Major Prophets*.

New International Version   A popular twentieth-century English translation of the Bible.

New Testament   "New Covenant" — The twenty-seven Bible books that tell of Jesus fulfilling and supplanting the "Old Covenant." They present the good news of forgiveness through faith in Jesus' death and resurrection.

Northern Kingdom   The ten tribes located north of Judah that split away from the heavy-handed rule of Solomon's son, Rehoboam, and formed their own nation (Israel). All the kings of Israel led their people in rebellion against God.

Old Testament   "Old Covenant" — The thirty-nine books of the Hebrew Bible.

Paraphrase   A version of the Bible that restates the literal rendering of the text into other words in an attempt to clarify meaning.

Pastoral Letters   Four New Testament letters (1 and 2 Timothy, Titus, Philemon) written by Paul to individual church leaders.

Pentecost   "Fiftieth" — A Jewish celebration held fifty days after Passover; the occasion on which the Holy Spirit empowered Jesus' followers (Acts 2).

Pharaoh   Title of the rulers (kings) of ancient Egypt.

Prophet   A person chosen and empowered by God to tell his message.

Protestant   An individual or church committed to the principles of the Protestant Reformation (1500s), including acceptance of the Bible as the only source of God's revelation, justification by faith alone, and the priesthood of all believers.

Psalms   Songs or poems, often prayers, usually expressing deep feelings about God; a Bible book containing 150 psalms.

Rabbi   "Teacher" — In the New Testament, this title is sometimes used of Jesus, and refers to his teaching ministry.

Resurrection   Return to life after death. Jesus' resurrection demonstrated his power over sin.

Roman Catholic   "Catholic" means universal. "Roman" refers to the church being headquartered in Rome. The Roman Catholic church was the dominant church until the Protestant Reformation in the 1500s.

Sanhedrin   The Jewish court for both religious and political affairs that functioned under the authority of the Roman governor.

Satrap   A ruler in ancient Persia.

Scribe   An expert in the Jewish law; a skilled writer or copyist.

Scripture   "Writing" — The Bible, both Old and New Testaments.

Septuagint   "Seventy" — The oldest Greek translation of the Hebrew Bible, completed by about seventy translators in Alexandria, Egypt, between 260 and 100 B.C. This was the version often quoted by New Testament writers and used by the early church.

Sin   Any action, attitude, or thought that opposes God's plan. Christ died to save us from the damages caused by our sin.

Southern Kingdom   The two tribes (Judah and Benjamin) that remained loyal to Solomon's son, Rehoboam, when the ten northern tribes formed their own nation (Israel). Judah had several godly kings and outlasted Israel by about 150 years.

Study Bible   A Bible that contains additional information (cross references, concordance, footnotes, etc.) to help the reader study it.

Synagogue   "Assembly" — A place where Jews gather to study the Hebrew Bible and worship. Synagogues were established after the exile and have become the active centers of Jewish life in any community where Jews live.

Synoptic Gospels   "See together" — The first three Gospels are called the Synoptics because they share a similar point of view on the life of Jesus and tell many of the same incidents.

Tabernacle   A large tent Moses and the people built at Mt. Sinai. It remained the central place of Israel's worship until Solomon built the temple in Jerusalem.

Temple   Solomon built the temple as the first permanent place for God's people to worship. The temple was destroyed and rebuilt twice. It was not rebuilt after the Romans destroyed it in A.D. 64.

The Message   A twentieth-century paraphrase of the New Testament that casts the meaning in contemporary words and phrases.

Torah   "Instruction" — The first five books of the Hebrew Bible.

Translation   A book or other communication that has been rephrased into a language other than the original.

Verse   A small segment of a Bible passage. Chapters are subdivided into verses. The chapter and verse designations were added long after the Bible was written to help readers locate passages quickly.

Version   A specific Bible translation (e.g., *The King James Version*, *The New International Version*).

Vulgate   "Common" — A fourth-century Latin translation of the Bible. By that time Latin had supplanted Greek as the common ("vulgar") language of the Mediterranean world.

The Bible:
Easy Access Guide

"Your word, O Lord, is eternal; it stands firm in the heavens."
"How sweet are your words to my taste, sweeter than honey to my mouth!"
"Your word is a lamp to my feet and a light for my path."
Psalm 119: 89, 103, 105

WHERE DO I START?

With most books, this question never comes up. Obviously, the place to start is at the beginning. However, since the Bible is a collection of sixty-six separate books, you have many more options in deciding what to read first. Your choice may be influenced by your reason for wanting to read the Bible:

OBJECTIVE	GOOD STARTING PLACE
Scan Bible history	Genesis (first book; stories of creation, flood, Abraham, Isaac, Jacob, Joseph)
Examine Jesus' life	Mark (second book in New Testament; shortest of four accounts of Jesus' life)
Study Jesus' teaching	John (fourth book in New Testament, emphasis on Jesus' words)
Build Christian life	1 John (short letter near end of Bible, practical instructions)
More prayer and praise	Psalms (150 songs and poems)

Further suggestions for choosing what to study are provided inside this booklet.

FINDING YOUR WAY AROUND

Thumbing through a Bible's pages can be intimidating. The Bible is long, and many of the names of books are unfamiliar and hard to pronounce. Here are a few tips to easily locate a place in the Bible.

Know the "Address"

The Bible has been meticulously subdivided so that almost every sentence has its own unique "address" or reference. Three pieces of information are consistently used in referring to any location in the Bible:

Book Name — The name of one of the sixty-six Bible books (e.g., Genesis, Psalms, Mark).

Chapter — Most Bible books (except for several very short ones) are divided into chapters. Chapter numbers appear at the top of each page and in large type within the text.

Verse — All chapters are divided into verses. A verse can be a sentence or part of a sentence. Verse numbers appear in small type in the body of the text.

Bible references are written with the book name, then the chapter and verse numbers separated by a colon. One of the most famous Bible references is John 3:16, meaning, the book of John, chapter 3, verse 16.

Use the Contents Page(s)

Every Bible has a contents page near the front of the Bible. The standard format is to list all the books of the Bible in the order the books appear, showing the thirty-nine Old Testament books first, then the twenty-seven New Testament books. *(See back page for a complete summary.)* Some Bibles also have an alphabetical contents page, listing all the books in order by name. This makes it easy to quickly locate a book in the list if you are unfamiliar with its general position in the Bible.

Divide and Locate

Besides using the contents page of the Bible to locate references, there is a quick way to open the Bible at or near the reference you want to find.

- Start from the front to get to one of the five books of the law.
- Divide the first quarter of the Bible's pages from those that follow to find yourself near the end of the books of history (probably 1 or 2 Samuel).
- Divide the Bible in half to open in the books of poetry (probably Psalms or Proverbs).
- Divide the last quarter of the Bible's pages to open near the start of the New Testament (Matthew).
- Start from the back to find Revelation or the general epistles.

Obviously, a Bible with a substantial number of additional pages in the front or back (e.g., preface, introduction, concordance, maps) will skew this process slightly.

CHOOSING WHAT TO STUDY

Pray About Your Bible Reading Plans

Take time to talk to God about how he can talk to you through his Word. Be open and honest with him about any barriers you may be facing (crowded schedule, limited Bible knowledge, lack of discipline, personal doubts, etc.). Ask for his guidance and help as you seek to learn more about him through his Word.

Become Part of a Bible Study Group

Most people find that group study provides a great deal of help in pursuing personal Bible study Even if the group is not currently focusing on the area of your greatest interest, the support and encouragement of a group can make it worthwhile to postpone your own individualized reading goals temporarily.

- Find out what Bible study options are available through your church, then get involved with one.

- Talk to the leader or others in the group for tips on Bible passages to read between group meetings.
- If your pastor is presenting a sermon series, find out what passages you could read that parallel each week's topic.

Set Aside Time for Bible Reading and Prayer

You are not likely to *find* time in the middle of a busy schedule to pick up your Bible and start reading. You need to look at your calendar and *set aside* time. For many people, scheduling the same time period each day works best, thereby building Bible reading into their daily routine. Others find it works better for them to schedule different time periods depending on each day's activities. The important thing is to be realistic and consistent.

Define a Bible Reading Plan You Can Follow

Avoid the temptation to start with plans you may not be able to carry out. Start with brief, simple passages, then gradually work your way to longer, more challenging parts of Scripture. It is better to read, think about, understand, and apply just one verse, than to "cover" chapters without putting truth into practice. "A One-Month Introduction to Your Bible" in this booklet is a good plan for getting started.

Focus on Today, Not on the Past

Whatever part of Scripture you study, knowing the original setting and purpose of a Bible book is important. However, historical knowledge is not the ultimate goal. The true purpose of God's Word has always been to guide us in how we live our lives. Here are a few tips to help.

GAIN BENEFIT FROM WHAT YOU READ

- Pray before and after you read. The Bible is God's Word, so ask him for help to understand and apply it.
- Read any passages both before and after a group study. You get more out of the group meeting if you read the passages first,